GCSE AQA
Biology
The Workbook

This book is for anyone doing **GCSE AQA Biology**.
It covers everything you'll need for your year 10 and 11 exams.

It's full of **tricky questions**... each one designed to make you **sweat** — because that's the only way you'll get any **better**.

There are questions to see **what facts** you know. There are questions to see how well you can **apply those facts**. And there are questions to see what you know about **how science works**.

It's also got some daft bits in to try and make the whole experience at least vaguely entertaining for you.

What CGP is all about

Our sole aim here at CGP is to produce the highest quality books — carefully written, immaculately presented and dangerously close to being funny.

Then we work our socks off to get them out to you — at the cheapest possible prices.

Contents

Biology 1a — Human Biology

Biology 1b — Environment and Evolution

Biology 2a — Cells, Organs and Populations

Biology 2b — Enzymes and Genetics

Biology 3a — Life Processes

Biology 3b — Humans and Their Environment

Published by CGP

Editors:
Charlotte Burrows, Mary Falkner, Ben Fletcher, Rosie McCurrie.

Contributors:
Jane Davies, James Foster, Paddy Gannon, Dr Iona MJ Hamilton, Rebecca Harvey, Kate Redmond, Adrian Schmit, Dee Wyatt.

ISBN: 978 1 84762 676 9

With thanks to Helen Brace, Janet Cruse-Sawyer, Ben Fletcher, James Foster, David Hickinson, Glenn Rogers and Karen Wells for the proofreading.
With thanks to Laura Jakubowski for the copyright research.

Data on page 19 supplied by the HFEA. The information collected and published by the HFEA is a snapshot of data provided by licensed clinics at a particular time.

Graph of sulfur dioxide emissions on page 34 & data on page 131, source ww2.defra.gov.uk © Crown copyright reproduced under the terms of the Click-Use licence.

DDT diagram on page 35 from Biological Science Combined Volume Hardback, 1990, Soper, Green, Stout, Taylor. Cambridge University Press.

Table of Kidney Failure Statistics on page 118 reproduced with permission from the NHS UK Transplant. www.organdonation.nhs.uk

Graph of average surface temperature of Earth on page 132 © Crown copyright 1995, published by the Met Office.

With thanks to the Intergovernmental Panel on Climate Change for permission to reproduce the graph of atmospheric gas concentrations used on page 132.

Every effort has been made to locate copyright holders and obtain permission to reproduce sources. For those sources where it has been difficult to trace the originator of the work, we would be grateful for information. If any copyright holder would like us to make an amendment to the acknowledgements, please notify us and we will gladly update the book at the next reprint. Thank you.

Groovy website: www.cgpbooks.co.uk

Printed by Elanders Ltd, Newcastle upon Tyne.
Jolly bits of clipart from CorelDRAW®
Based on the classic CGP style created by Richard Parsons.

Diet and Metabolic Rate

Q1 Tick the box next to the correct definition of a **healthy diet**.

- [ ] A diet containing protein, carbohydrates, fibre, vitamins and minerals but no sugar or fat.
- [ ] A diet containing the right balance of different foods and the right amount of energy.
- [ ] A diet containing equal amounts of protein, carbohydrates, fats, fibre, vitamins and minerals.

Q2 Complete the following sentences to show the functions in the body of different food groups.

a) Protein is needed for .... and ....

b) Carbohydrates provide much of your ....

c) Fats are needed to .... and for ....

d) Vitamins and minerals are needed in .... amounts to stay healthy.

Q3 Answer the following questions about **metabolism**.

a) Explain what is meant by the term 'metabolic rate'.

....

....

b) Circle **three** factors from the list below that will affect a person's metabolic rate.

proportion of muscle to fat in the body

proportion of hair to bone in the body

inherited factors

amount of exercise

number of brothers and sisters

Q4 Wendy and June both work as IT technicians. Wendy is training to run a marathon and goes to the gym every evening. June doesn't enjoy sport and prefers playing chess in her spare time. Who needs more **protein** and **carbohydrate** in their diet — June or Wendy? Explain your answer.

....

....

....

Top Tips: Mmm, what I couldn't do with 6000 Calories per day... Anyway, remember that everyone needs a balanced diet, but not everyone needs to eat exactly the same stuff.

Diet and Metabolic Rate

Q5 Different people need to eat **different amounts** of food because they have different energy requirements.

Calories are a measure of the amount of energy in food.

a) It is recommended that the average woman eats about 2000 Calories per day, while the average man should eat about 2500 Calories. Explain why there is a difference.

....

....

b) Cyclists riding in the Tour de France bike race need to eat about 6000 Calories per day during the race. This is more than twice what the average man requires. Explain why.

....

....

Q6 The bar chart shows the proportions of each **food group** that make up three different foods.

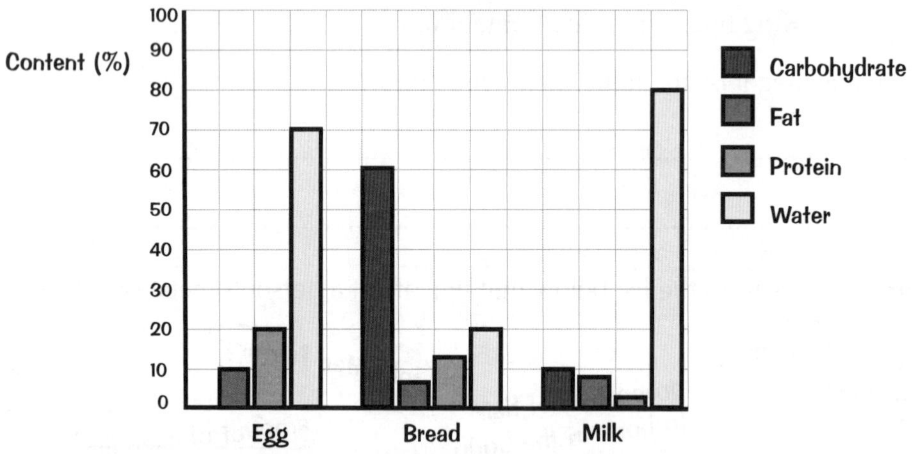

Content (%)
100
90
80
70
60
50
40
30
20
10
0
Egg
Bread
Milk
Carbohydrate
Fat
Protein
Water

a) Which food contains the highest proportion of fat? ....

b) What is the difference between the amount of carbohydrate in 50 g of bread and the amount of carbohydrate in 50 g of milk? Give your answer in grams and show your working out.

....

....

The % in the bar chart is like the no. of grams you'd have in 100 g of the food.

c) For my lunch I have scrambled eggs on toast and a glass of milk. Suggest another food I could have to make this a more balanced meal. Explain your answer.

....

....

Factors Affecting Health

Q1 A person may have poor health due to being **malnourished**.

a) What do we mean when we say a person is 'malnourished'?

....

b) Deficiency diseases are often associated with malnutrition. What is a deficiency disease?

....

Q2 How can a person be both **'fit'** and **malnourished**?

....

....

Q3 Fifty men and fifty women were asked whether they thought they were **obese**.
Each was then given a medical examination to **check** whether they were actually obese.

	Thought they were obese	Actually obese
No. of women	9	16
No. of men	5	11

a) What percentage of women in this survey were obese? ....

b) What are the most common causes of obesity in developed countries?

....

c) Underline any health problems in the list below that have been linked to obesity.

heart disease **hepatitis** **influenza** **cancers** **scurvy** **type 2 diabetes**

Q4 Answer the following questions about **health**.

a) Why are people who exercise regularly usually healthier than people who don't?

....

....

b) Give **two** ways in which inherited factors can affect a person's health.

....

Evaluating Food, Lifestyle and Diet

Q1 Circle the correct words to complete this passage on **weight loss**.

To lose body mass, a person needs to take in **more** / **less** energy than they **use** / **store**.

Eating **more** / **less** fat and carbohydrate means the body takes in less energy.

Exercise **increases** / **decreases** the amount of energy used by the body.

Q2 Two reports on **low-fat foods** were published on one day. **Report A** appeared in a tabloid paper. It said that the manufacturers of 'Crunchie Bites' have shown that the latest girl band, Kandyfloss, lost weight using their product. **Report B** appeared in a *Journal of Medicine* and reported how 6000 volunteers lost weight during a trial of an experimental medicine.

Which of these reports is likely to be the most reliable and why?

....

....

Q3 The **nutritional labels** of two different burgers are shown below. Both burgers have the **same weight**.

A:

NUTRITIONAL INFORMATION	per burger
Energy	2538 kJ
Protein	33 g
Carbohydrate	51 g
of which sugars	12 g
Fat	30 g
of which saturates	7 g
Fibre	2 g
Sodium	0.9 g

B:

NUTRITIONAL INFORMATION	per burger
Energy	2718 kJ
Protein	19 g
Carbohydrate	56 g
of which sugars	16 g
Fat	39 g
of which saturates	12 g
Fibre	1 g
Sodium	1.9 g

a) Which is the most **unhealthy** burger? Explain your answer.

....

....

b) Sharon eats burger B three times a week. She reads and goes to the theatre regularly, but doesn't do any kind of exercise. Explain how Sharon's choice of lifestyle could affect her health.

....

....

Fighting Disease

Q1 What is a **pathogen**?

....

....

Q2 Underline the correct description of an **antigen**.

A 'foreign' cell.

A chemical that causes disease.

A molecule that destroys bacteria.

A molecule that causes an immune response.

Q3 Decide whether the following statements are **true** or **false**.

		True	False
a)	Some pathogens can make you feel very ill.	☐	☐
b)	Infectious diseases can be passed on genetically.	☐	☐
c)	All pathogens are bacteria.	☐	☐
d)	Infectious diseases are not caused by living organisms.	☐	☐
e)	Some pathogens can be spread between organisms very easily.	☐	☐

Q4 Fill in the gaps in the passage below using the words in the box.

small	bursts	cells	damaging	toxins	damage	poisons	copies

Bacteria are .... organisms which can multiply rapidly inside the body. Some can make you ill by .... your body cells or producing .... (..).

Viruses are tiny particles — they are not .... Viruses replicate by fooling body cells into making .... of them. The cell then .... and releases the new virus. This cell .... makes you feel ill.

Fighting Disease

Q5 The body has several methods of **defending itself** against the entry of **pathogens**.
Below are examples of how some bacterial pathogens can enter the body.
In each case, describe how your body prevents against illness.

a) *Staphylococcus aureus* can cause blood poisoning by getting into the blood through cuts.

....

....

b) *Streptococcus pneumoniae* can enter the body from the air as a person breathes.

....

....

Q6 **White blood cells** protect the body from infection.

a) Give **three** ways that they do this.

....

....

....

b) Some white blood cells can produce antibodies to deal with invading microorganisms.
Can an antibody recognise a wide range of microorganisms? Explain your answer.

....

....

Q7 If you have already had chickenpox you will usually be **immune** to the disease and will not suffer any symptoms if you are exposed to the infection again. Explain why this is.

....

....

....

Top Tips: Pathogens are all nasty little blighters that can make you ill if they manage to get inside you. Luckily, your body has a few handy ways of defending itself — make sure you remember all of them. And don't get your antigens, antibodies and antitoxins mixed up, whatever you do...

Fighting Disease — Vaccination

Q1 Circle the correct words to complete the passage below.

> Illness can be due to microorganisms **dying** / **causing damage** before the immune system can destroy them. If you become infected with a microorganism you have been vaccinated against, you **will** / **won't** have specific antibodies in your blood before the infection.

Q2 **Vaccination** involves injecting dead or inactive microorganisms into the body.

a) Tick the correct boxes to say whether the statements about vaccinations are **true** or **false**.

	True	False
i) The injected microorganisms have the same antigens as the live pathogen.	☐	☐
ii) White blood cells produce antibodies against the antigens on the injected microorganisms.	☐	☐
iii) After a vaccination, the white bloods cells can produce antibodies to fight all kinds of diseases.	☐	☐
iv) Vaccinations can wear off over time.	☐	☐

b) Why are dead or inactive microorganisms used in vaccinations?

....

Q3 A **vaccination programme** was introduced in a country to stop the spread of **disease A**. Parents were advised to have their children vaccinated at the age of 3. Two years later, a survey was done to see the effects of the vaccination programme. The results obtained are shown below.

> **Of the children vaccinated, 11% had developed the disease.**
> **Of the non-vaccinated children, 40% had developed the disease.**
> **Of the vaccinated children, 10% suffered side effects.**
> **In 3 cases, the side effects of the vaccination were very serious.**

Underline any of the statements below that are **possible** explanations for the fact that the injection worked for some and not others.

The vaccine does not work.

The vaccine did not work in some cases because the children had previously suffered from the disease.

The children who did not get the disease were in better general health.

You are not expected to know the facts in questions like this – they're just to test your judgement about scientific issues.

Fighting Disease — Vaccination

Q4 John gets injected with the **tuberculosis (TB) vaccine** but James doesn't. Soon afterwards both boys are exposed to the TB virus. Explain why James gets ill but John **doesn't**.

....

....

....

....

Q5 The **MMR vaccine** has a small risk of serious **side effects**, including meningitis or convulsions. However, the Government recommends that **all** children are given the MMR vaccine.

a) Which diseases does the MMR vaccine protect against?

....

b) Give **one** reason why the Government still recommends that all children are given the MMR vaccine.

....

....

Q6 Answer these questions about **vaccination**.

a) Describe how vaccinations have changed the pattern of disease in the UK.

....

....

b) Describe **two** problems that occasionally occur with vaccines.

....

....

....

Top Tips: Vaccination is a really effective way of controlling the spread of disease. And if most of the population is vaccinated against a specific disease, this reduces the chances of an epidemic.

Fighting Disease — Drugs

Q1 A new medicine called 'Killcold' contains **painkillers** and **decongestants**.

a) Explain why its name isn't strictly accurate.

....

....

b) Why don't doctors give antibiotics for colds?

....

....

c) Why is it more difficult to develop drugs to destroy viruses than it is to develop drugs to kill bacteria?

....

....

d) Why is it important for a doctor to prescribe the right type of antibiotic for an infection?

....

....

Q2 The graph shows the number of bacteria in Gary's blood during a two-week course of **antibiotics**.

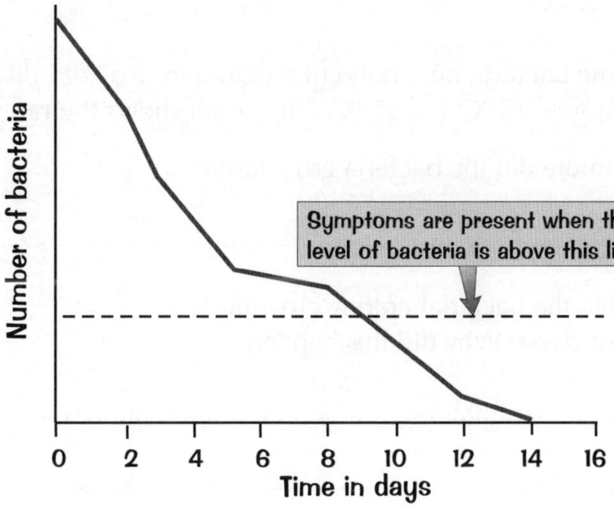

a) How long after starting the course of antibiotics did Gary's symptoms disappear? ....

b) Explain why Gary was probably suffering from something **more serious** than a sore throat.

....

....

Fighting Disease — Drugs

Q3 a) Write numbers in the boxes below to show the **order** the statements should be in to explain how bacteria become resistant to antibiotics. The first one has been done for you.

- [1] Bacteria mutate and sometimes the mutations cause them to be resistant to an antibiotic.
- [ ] The population of the resistant strain of bacteria will increase.
- [ ] When you treat the infection, only the non-resistant strains of bacteria will be killed.
- [ ] The individual resistant bacteria will survive and reproduce.
- [ ] So if you have an infection, some of the bacteria might be resistant to antibiotics.

b) Name **one** type of bacterium that has developed resistance to antibiotics.

....

Q4 **Microorganisms** can be **grown** in the laboratory on a Petri dish to investigate the effect of antibiotics and disinfectants. Explain why:

a) A lid should be kept on the Petri dish before and after the microorganisms are added.

....

b) The microorganisms should be transferred using an inoculating loop which has been passed through a flame.

....

Q5 A scientist grew some **bacteria** on a nutrient medium in two Petri dishes. He kept the two dishes at different temperatures, 25 °C and 37 °C. The graph shows the **rates of growth** of the bacteria.

a) i) At which temperature did the bacteria grow faster?

....

ii) What happened to the bacterial colony growing at 37 °C after four days? Why did this happen?

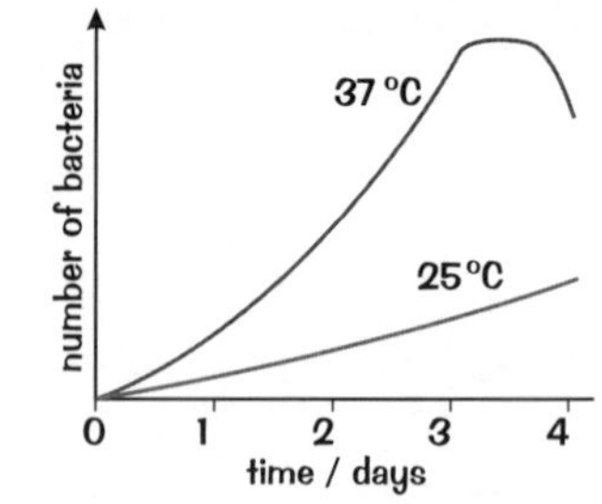

....

....

b) Suggest why the scientist chose 37 °C as one of the temperatures in his experiment.

....

c) Explain why Petri dishes are usually incubated at 25 °C in school experiments.

....

Fighting Disease — Past and Future

Q1 Ignaz Semmelweis worked in a hospital in Vienna in the 1840s. The graph shows the percentage of women dying after childbirth, before and after a **change** that he made.

a) What was the change and why did it help?

....

....

....

% of women dying after childbirth
12
10
8
6
4
2
before
after

b) After Semmelweis left, the doctors went back to their old ways. Why do you think this was?

....

....

Q2 **Antibiotics** were discovered in the 1940s.

a) Describe what has happened to the number of deaths from infectious bacterial diseases since the introduction of antibiotics.

....

b) Antibiotic-resistant strains of bacteria are becoming more common.

i) Give **one** example of how humans have increased the rate of development of resistant strains.

....

ii) Give **one** way that drug companies are trying to tackle the problem of resistant strains of bacteria.

....

Q3 Some bacteria and viruses **evolve quickly**.

a) Give **two** reasons why a new strain of bacteria could spread very rapidly in a population of people.

....

....

b) A new strain of bacteria could cause an epidemic. What is an epidemic?

....

c) It can be difficult to find an effective **vaccine** against diseases caused by pathogens that evolve rapidly. Explain why.

....

....

The Nervous System

Q1 Suggest why it is important for animals to be able to **detect changes** in their surroundings.

....

Q2 **Tick** the box next to the correct statement below.

☐ Light receptor cells contain a nucleus, cytoplasm and a cell wall.

☐ Light receptor cells have the same structures as plant cells.

☐ Light receptor cells contain a nucleus, cytoplasm and a cell membrane.

Q3 Which of the following is **not** an example of a **stimulus**? Underline your answer.

pressure **hearing** **chemical** **change in body position** **change in temperature**

Q4 In each sentence below, underline the **sense organ** involved and write down the **type of receptor** that is detecting the stimulus.

a) Tariq puts a piece of lemon on his tongue. The lemon tastes sour.

....

b) Siobhan wrinkles her nose as she smells something unpleasant in her baby brother's nappy.

....

c) Xabi's ears were filled with the sound of the crowd cheering his outstanding goal.

....

d) Lindsey feels a wasp sting the skin on the back of her neck. She screams very loudly.

....

Q5 Some parts of the body are known as the **CNS**.

a) What do the letters CNS stand for? ....

b) Name the two main parts of the CNS.

1. .... 2. ....

c) What type of cell carries information to and from the CNS? ....

The Nervous System

Q6 Explain why a man with a **damaged spinal cord** may not be able to feel someone touching his toe.

....

....

....

Q7 John and Marc investigated how **sensitive** different parts of the body are to **pressure**.

They stuck two pins in a cork 0.5 cm apart. The pins were placed on different parts of the body. Ten pupils took part — they were blindfolded and reported "yes" or "no" to feeling both points.

The results of the experiment are shown in the table.

Area of the body tested	Number of pupils reporting 'yes'
Sole of foot	2
Knee	3
Fingertip	10
Back of hand	5
Lip	9

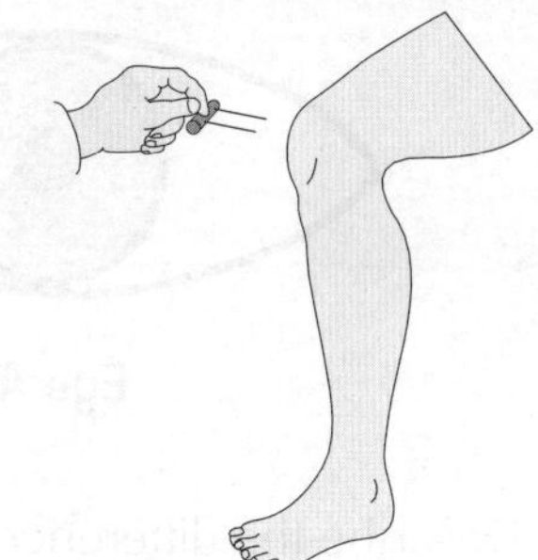

a) Which part of the body do the results suggest is:

i) most sensitive? .... **ii)** least sensitive? ....

b) From the results above, which part of the body do you think contains the **most pressure receptors**? Explain your answer.

....

....

c) John and Marc took it in turns to test the pupils. Their teacher suggested that if only one of the boys had done all the testing, the experiment would have been fairer. Explain why.

....

....

d) Each pupil was tested once. Suggest how you might make the test more accurate.

....

....

Synapses and Reflexes

Q1 **Circle** the correct answer to complete each of the following sentences.

a) Reflexes happen more **quickly** / **slowly** than considered responses.

b) The **vertebrae** / **spinal cord** can coordinate a reflex response.

c) The main purpose of a reflex is to **protect** / **display** the body.

d) Reflexes happen **with** / **without** you thinking about them.

e) Cells called **receptors** / **sense organs** detect stimuli.

f) A synapse is a connection between two **effectors** / **neurones**.

g) **Chemicals** / **Impulses** are released at synapses.

Q2 Look carefully at the diagrams showing two different **eyes** below.

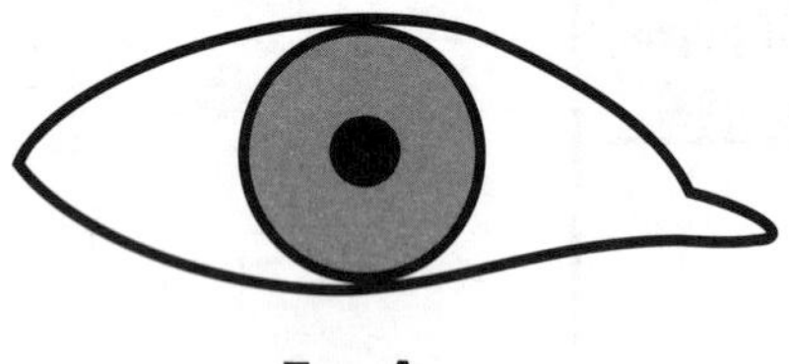

Eye A

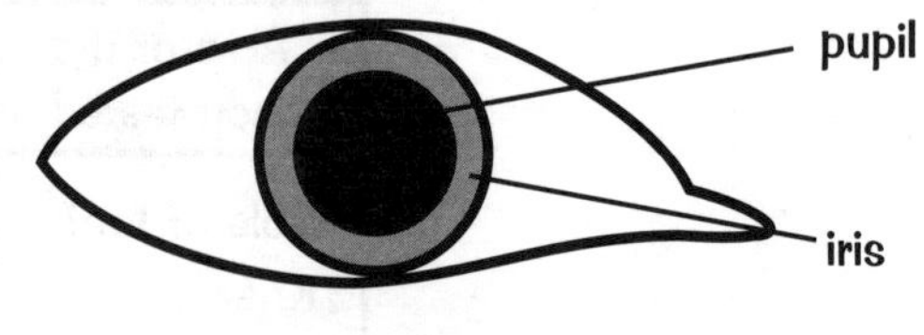

Eye B

a) Describe the difference you can see in the appearance of the two eyes.

....

....

b) Which diagram do you think shows an eye in bright light? Explain your answer.

....

....

c) Is the response illustrated by the diagrams above a voluntary or automatic response?

....

d) Explain why it is an advantage to have this type of response controlling the action of the eye.

....

....

....

Synapses and Reflexes

Q3 Why is a **reflex** reaction faster than a **voluntary** reaction?

Q4 When you touch something hot with a finger you **automatically** pull the finger away. The diagram shows some parts of the nervous system involved in this **reflex action**.

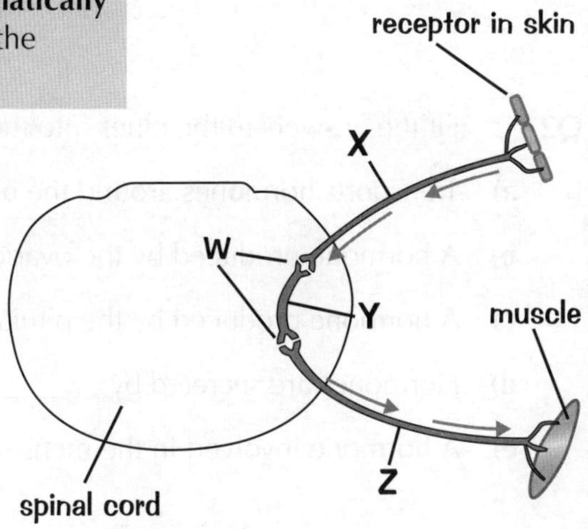

a) What type of neurone is:

i) neurone **X**? ....

ii) neurone **Y**? ....

iii) neurone **Z**? ....

b) In what form is the information carried:

i) along neurone **X**?

ii) from neurone **X** to neurone **Y**?

c) **i)** Complete the sentence.

In this reflex action the muscle acts as the ....

ii) Briefly describe how the muscle responds in this example.

d) **i)** What are the gaps marked **W** on the diagram called?

ii) Explain how the impulses get across these gaps.

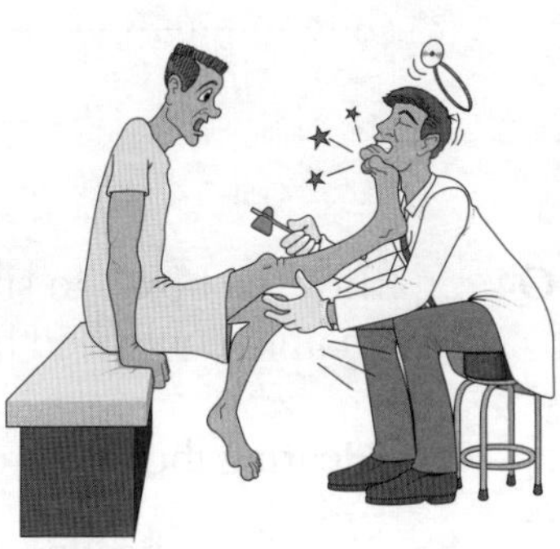

Top Tips: You could be asked about any kind of reflex in the exam. But just remember, they always involve the same reflex arc — stimulus, receptor, sensory neurone, relay neurone, motor neurone, effector, response. So once you've learnt it, you can apply your knowledge to anything.

Hormones

Q1 Complete the passage below about **hormones**.

Hormones are .... messengers. They are produced in .... and released into the .... They are carried all around the body, but only affect certain .... cells.

Q2 Fit the answers to the clues into the **grid**.

a) Transports hormones around the body.

b) A hormone produced by the ovaries.

c) A hormone produced by the pituitary.

d) Hormones are secreted by ____________.

e) A hormone involved in the menstrual cycle.

Q3 Describe the major differences between responses brought about by **hormones** and those due to the **nervous system**.

....

....

....

....

Q4 Tick the boxes to show whether the following responses are mainly controlled by the **nervous** or **hormonal** systems.

	Nervous system	Hormonal system
a) Hearing the alarm clock and turning it off.	☐	☐
b) Your heart beating faster when you remember you have an exam that day.	☐	☐
c) Smelling toast burning.	☐	☐
d) Your hairs standing on end when you're cold.	☐	☐
e) The 'fight-or-flight' response.	☐	☐

The Menstrual Cycle

Q1 There are three main **hormones** involved in the menstrual cycle.

Complete the table to show **where** in the body each hormone is produced.

HORMONE	WHERE IT IS PRODUCED
FSH	
oestrogen	
LH	

Q2 **FSH**, **LH** and **oestrogen** have specific functions in the menstrual cycle.

a) Describe **two** functions of FSH.

1. ....

2. ....

b) What effect does oestrogen have on the production of FSH?

....

c) Describe the function of LH.

....

Q3 The diagram below shows how the **uterus lining** changes during the **menstrual cycle**.

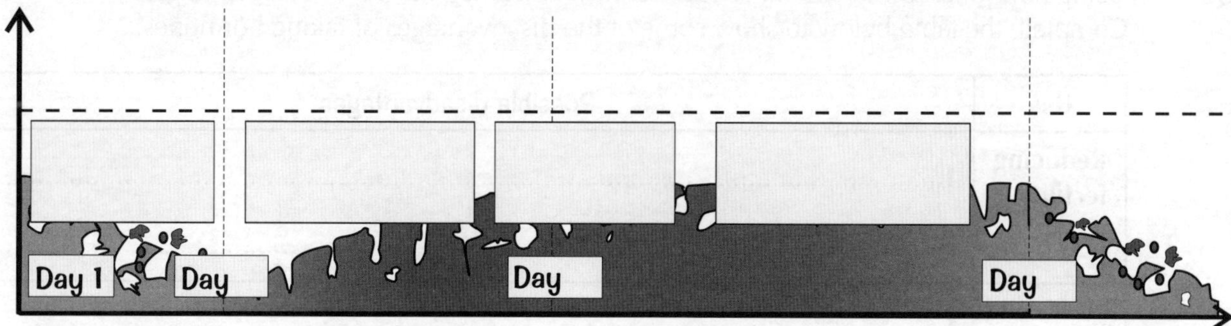

a) Fill in the day numbers in the boxes where they are missing.

b) Fill in the remaining boxes using the labels below:

Uterus lining builds up

Egg released

Uterus lining maintained

Uterus lining breaks down

Controlling Fertility

Q1 Hormones can be used to **increase fertility**.

a) Underline **two** hormones from the list below that can be taken by a woman to increase her fertility.

FSH oestrogen insulin LH progesterone

b) Briefly explain how these hormones increase fertility.

....

Q2 The **combined pill** contains oestrogen and progesterone.

a) State **two** benefits of taking the combined pill.

....

....

b) Explain how oestrogen in the pill reduces fertility.

....

....

....

c) Suggest why a woman might take a progesterone-only pill, rather than the combined pill.

....

Q3 Using hormones to increase or reduce fertility in women has some **disadvantages**. Complete the table below to show some of the disadvantages of taking hormones.

Use	Possible disadvantages
Reducing fertility	1.. 2..
Increasing fertility	1.. 2..

Top Tips: Sometimes, it's haaard to be... a womaaan... Or a man, if you're trying to learn all this. You also need to know that hormones which increase fertility are called fertility drugs, whereas hormones that reduce fertility are called contraceptive drugs.

Controlling Fertility

Q4 Describe how the **level of hormones** in the combined pill has changed since it was first developed, and explain why.

....

....

Q5 **In vitro fertilisation** can help couples to have children.

a) Explain how **in vitro fertilisation** works.

....

....

....

b) Discuss the advantages and disadvantages of in vitro fertilisation.

....

....

....

Q6 The graph shows the **percentage success rates** of **IVF treatment** for women in the UK in 2007.

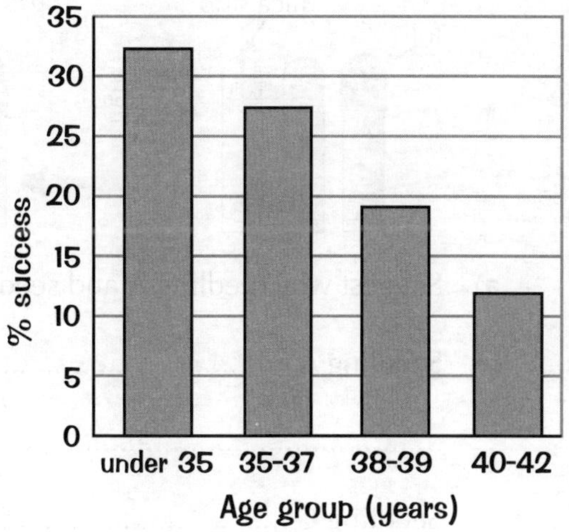

a) What was the % success rate in women aged 35–37?

....

b) What conclusion can be drawn about the effect of a woman's age on the success of IVF treatment?

....

....

....

c) IVF treatment is expensive, but for some couples the costs are paid by the National Health Service. From the graph, suggest **one** reason why the NHS might decide not to pay for IVF treatment for women over 40.

....

Plant Hormones

Q1 Decide whether the following statements are **true** or **false**.

		True	False
a)	Plant shoots grow away from light.	☐	☐
b)	Plant roots grow towards light.	☐	☐
c)	Plant roots grow in the same direction that gravity acts.	☐	☐
d)	If the tip of a shoot is removed, the shoot may stop growing upwards.	☐	☐
e)	Phototropism is the growth of a plant in response to moisture.	☐	☐
f)	Geotropism (gravitropism) is the growth of a plant in response to gravity.	☐	☐

Q2 Choose the **correct word** or **phrase** from each pair to complete the following paragraph.

When a shoot tip is exposed to light from one side, auxin accumulates on the side that's in the **light** / **shade**. This makes the cells grow **faster** / **slower** on the shaded side, so the shoot bends **away from** / **towards** the light. When a shoot is growing sideways, auxin accumulates on the **upper** / **lower** side. This makes the cells on that side grow **faster** / **slower**, bending the shoots **upwards** / **downwards**.

Q3 Vicky used three seedlings to investigate plant growth. Each seedling was prepared differently (see table). All three were placed in the same conditions, exposed to light from **one** direction and left for five hours. She recorded her results in the table below.

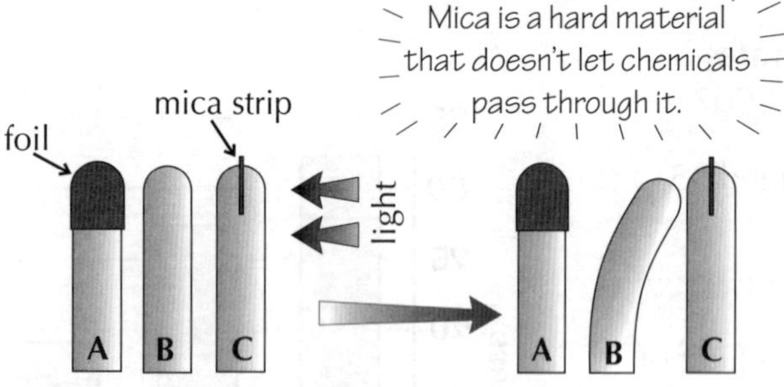

Seedling	Preparation	Observation after 5 hours
A	foil covering tip	no change
B	left alone	tip bent towards the light
C	mica strip through centre of tip	no change

a) Suggest why seedling A and seedling C failed to respond to the light.

Seedling A ....

....

Seedling C ....

....

b) Suggest how the experiment could be improved.

....

Plant Hormones

Q4 Sanjay owns two neighbouring fields — **Field A** and **Field B**. They are an identical size, have the same soil and he uses the same fertiliser regime for both. The only difference is that he applies a weedkiller containing plant growth hormones to Field B but not Field A.

This table shows the yields for both fields.

Year	1997	1998	1999	2000	2001
Barley yield from field A, kg/ha	35	28	33	37	34
Barley yield from field B, kg/ha	48	39	44	49	43

a) What effect did the weedkiller have on crop yield?

....

b) Explain how this type of weedkiller works.

....

....

Q5 Barry is investigating the effect of **auxin concentration** on the growth of the roots in some **identical plant cuttings**. His measurements are shown in the table.

Plant cuttings are pieces of plants that have been cut off to grow into new plants.

a) Complete the table by calculating the increase in root length at each concentration.

Concentration of auxin (parts per million)	0	0.001	0.01	0.1	1
Length of root at start of investigation (mm)	20	20	20	20	20
Length of root 1 week after investigation started (mm)	26	32	28	23	21
Increase of root length (mm)					

b) Plot a bar chart of the concentration of auxin against the increase in root length on the graph paper.

c) What do the results suggest is the best concentration of auxin to use to encourage growth?

....

d) What do you notice about the effect of high auxin concentration on the rate of growth?

....

....

e) Give one way in which Barry has helped to make this a fair test.

....

Homeostasis

Q1 Define **homeostasis**.

....

....

Q2 The human body is usually maintained at a temperature of about **37 °C**.

a) Why do humans suffer ill effects if their body temperature varies too much from this temperature?

....

....

b) Which part of your body monitors your body temperature to ensure that it is kept constant?

....

Q3 The graph shows the **blood sugar level** of a healthy person over a period of 5 hours.

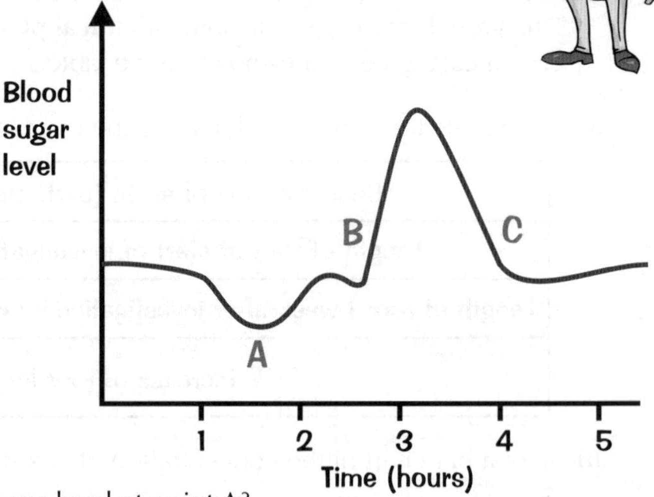

Blood sugar level

B C

A

1 2 3 4 5

Time (hours)

a) What might have caused the drop in blood sugar level at point A?

....

b) The blood sugar level rose quickly at point B. What could have caused this increase in sugar level?

....

c) Why does the body's blood sugar level need to be constantly maintained?

....

Top Tips: Homeostasis is a collective term for lots of different processes going on in lots of different parts of the body. What they all have in common is that they're trying to keep various things as constant and steady as possible — be it temperature, water content, blood sugar, ion content...

Homeostasis

Q4 Choose the **correct words** to complete the paragraph below.

On a **cold** / **hot** day or when you're exercising, you **sweat a lot** / **don't sweat much**, so you will produce **more** / **less** urine. The urine will be a **pale** / **dark** colour as it contains **less** / **more** water than usual. We say that the urine is more **concentrated** / **dilute** than usual.

Q5 Ronald eats a meal that is very high in **salt**. Which of the answers below explain correctly how Ronald's body gets rid of this excess salt? Tick one or more boxes.

- [ ] Ronald's liver removes salt from his blood.
- [ ] Ronald loses salt in his sweat.
- [ ] Ronald's kidneys remove salt from his blood.
- [ ] Ronald's saliva becomes more salty, and the salt is lost when he breathes.
- [ ] Ronald gets rid of salt in his urine.

Q6 Let's suppose I put my annoying uncle on a treadmill and turn the setting to high (just to keep him quiet for a bit).*

Will my uncle lose **more** or **less** water from the following body parts than he would if he sat still? Explain your answers.

a) Skin ....

....

b) Lungs ....

....

c) Kidneys ....

....

Q7 Mrs Finnegan had the **concentration of ions** in her urine measured on two days.

Date	6th December	20th July
Average air temperature	8 °C	24 °C
Ion concentration in urine	1.5 mg/cm^3	2.1 mg/cm^3

Assuming Mrs Finnegan always eats exactly the same food every day, suggest a reason for the different ion concentrations in her urine.

....

....

* Don't try this at home (I got into trouble).

Drugs

Q1 a) What does the term 'drug' mean?

....

b) i) What does it mean if you are **addicted** to a drug?

....

....

ii) Give **one** example of a drug that is very addictive. ....

c) **Statins** are a prescribed drug. What are statins used for?

....

Q2 **Stimulants** are used by some athletes.

a) Why might an athlete use stimulants?

....

b) Give **two** ethical arguments against an athlete using stimulants.

....

....

Q3 Scientists are still **not sure** whether there is a link between using cannabis and developing mental health problems, despite the fact that lots of studies have been carried out. Explain why this is.

....

....

Q4 A drug trial involved 6000 patients with **high cholesterol levels**. 3000 patients were given **statins**, and 3000 were not. Both groups made lifestyle changes to try to lower their cholesterol, based on advice given. The decrease in the patients' cholesterol levels is shown on the graph.

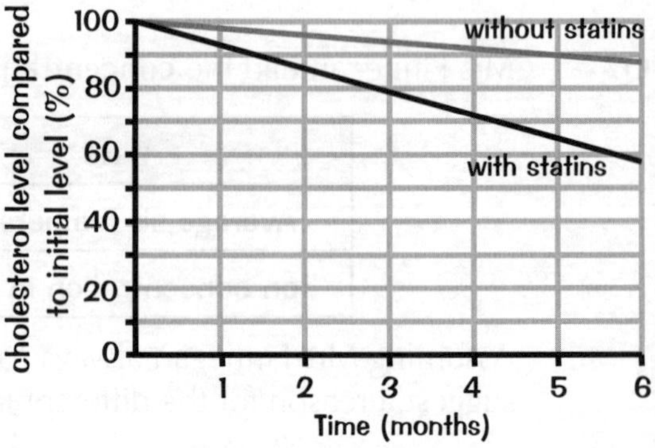

a) Why was the group without statins included?

....

b) Suggest a conclusion that can be drawn from these results. ....

....

Testing Medicinal Drugs

Q1 Write numbers in the boxes below to show the **correct order** in which drugs are tested.

☐ Drug is tested on live animals.

☐ Human volunteers are used to test the drug.

☐ Drug is tested on human cells and tissues.

Q2 Before drugs are made freely available, **clinical trials** must be performed.

a) Give **two** reasons why clinical trials have to be done before drugs are made freely available.

....

....

b) Briefly explain why a drug is tested on **healthy** volunteers first?

....

....

Q3 **Thalidomide** is a drug that was developed in the 1950s.

a) What was this drug originally developed for? ....

b) Thalidomide was not fully tested. What effect did it have when given to pregnant women?

....

....

c) Name **one** disease that thalidomide is now used in the treatment of. ....

Q4 A pharmaceutical company is trialling a new drug. They are using a **placebo** in the trial and are conducting the trials 'double blind'.

a) What is a placebo?

....

b) Why are the scientists using a placebo?

....

....

c) What is a double-blind trial?

....

....

Recreational Drugs

Q1 Look at the following examples of **health problems** and underline any that are related to **drinking alcohol**.

mumps   liver disease   addiction   lung disease   unconsciousness

Q2 Recreational drugs include **cannabis**, **ecstasy** and **heroin**.

a) Give **two reasons** why someone might use recreational drugs.

1. ....

2. ....

b) Give **one** negative effect that cannabis, ecstasy and heroin can have on the body.

....

Q3 There are three main opinions about the **link** between cannabis and hard drugs. Explain the idea behind each of the following:

a) Stepping stone:

....

b) Gateway drug:

....

c) Genetics:

....

Q4 The use of **legal drugs** causes lots of problems in this country.

a) Why do alcohol and smoking have a **bigger impact** than illegal drugs in the UK?

....

b) Give two ways in which misuse of alcohol and smoking **negatively** affect the **economy** in the UK.

....

....

Top Tips: You'd think it'd be the hard illegal drugs that cause the most damage to society — but it's the legal drugs, because of the huge numbers of people who take them. Remember this, so that you don't get caught out in the exam. Next up, a load of mixed questions just over the page. FUN.

Mixed Questions — Biology 1a

Q1 The diagram shows a runner waiting to start a race in the Olympic Games.

a) Give one sense organ that the athlete is relying on at the start of the race, and state the type of receptors it uses.

....

b) When the athlete starts the race, information will travel around his body via neurones.

i) What is the difference between motor neurones and sensory neurones?

....

ii) Explain how a nerve signal passes from one neurone to the next.

....

....

c) The athlete has trained hard for the race, but some of his competitors have taken **steroids**.

i) Why might an athlete use steroids?

....

ii) Give **one** negative health effect of using steroids.

....

Q2 The diagram represents the **menstrual cycle** in a particular woman.

0
menstrual period
5
10
15
Day 16
20
25

a) What is the length of the complete menstrual cycle shown?

.... days.

b) What happens on day 16 of this woman's cycle?

....

c) Oestrogen is one of the main hormones that control the menstrual cycle. Name another hormone involved.

....

d) Explain how the oestrogen in the contraceptive pill prevents pregnancy.

....

....

Mixed Questions — Biology 1a

Q3 a) Circle the best word or phrase from each pair to complete the sentences below.

i) **Carbohydrates** / **Vitamins** are needed in tiny amounts to keep you healthy.

ii) **Overeating** / **Undereating** can cause obesity.

iii) An overweight person usually has a **higher** / **lower** metabolic rate than an average person.

iv) A farmer is likely to need a lot **more** / **less** energy than someone working in a call centre.

v) Carbohydrates are broken down into sugars to provide **energy** / **materials to build new cells**.

b) Water is a vital part of our diet and the body's water level is controlled by homeostasis.

i) Name three ways that water is lost from the body.

....

ii) Explain why the amount of urine that people produce can depend on the air temperature.

....

....

Q4 Scientists spend a lot of time **researching** new diets and drugs.

a) Why are drugs tested on animals before they are used in clinical trials?

....

....

b) List three factors that can give you an indication of how reliable a scientific report is.

....

....

Q5 Tick the boxes below that are next to **true** statements.

Heroin is an example of an addictive, illegal drug. ☐

Alcohol doesn't tend to cause serious problems because it is legal. ☐

You can't get addicted to alcohol. ☐

Some studies have found a link between cannabis use and mental health problems. ☐

It has been proven that the desire to take cannabis and other drugs is genetic. ☐

Mixed Questions — Biology 1a

Q6 **Hormones** are chemical substances.

a) How do hormones travel around the body?

....

b) Tick all the factors below that describe how hormones work.

- ☐ slow response
- ☐ response lasts for a long time
- ☐ response lasts for a short time
- ☐ acts on a very precise area in the body

c) Plants contain hormones too.

i) Where in a plant is the hormone **auxin** produced?

....

ii) Describe the **difference** between how auxin affects cells in the shoots and in the roots of plants.

....

....

iii) Name **one** use of auxin in agriculture.

....

Q7 Gavin and Joan carried out an experiment at school to investigate the effectiveness of six different **antibiotics** (1-6). They grew some bacteria on a sterile agar plate. They then placed discs of filter paper, impregnated with the six different antibiotics, onto the bacterial culture.

The clear zone is where there's no bacterial growth.

a) What has happened in the **clear zone** labelled on the diagram?

....

....

....

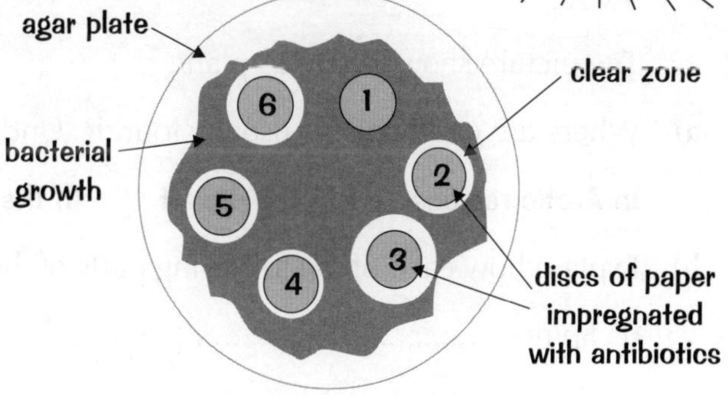

agar plate
clear zone
bacterial growth
1
2
3
4
5
6
discs of paper impregnated with antibiotics

b) **i)** Which of the antibiotics (1-6) was the **most effective** against these bacteria?

....

ii) Would this antibiotic also work against the flu, or a common cold? Explain your answer.

....

....

Adaptations

Q1 Pictures of a **polar bear** and a small rodent called a **kangaroo rat** are shown below.

Diagrams are not to scale.

a) Which of these animals do you think has the smallest body surface area? ....

b) Which animal has the smallest body surface area **compared to its volume**? ....

> This is a tricky one. Remember, long, thin shapes have a big surface area compared to their volume.

c) Explain how this animal's **shape** helps to reduce its body surface area compared to its volume.

....

d) Does having a **smaller** body surface area compared to volume mean that more or less **heat** can be lost from an animal's body?

....

e) The kangaroo rat lives in hot desert regions. Would you expect its body surface area compared to volume to be bigger or smaller than the polar bear's? Explain why.

....

....

....

Q2 The picture shows a **cactus** plant.

a) Where are cactus plants usually found? Underline the correct answer below.

In Arctic regions **In the desert** **In the mountains** **Near the sea**

b) Explain how each of the following parts of the cactus help it to survive in its normal habitat.

i) Spines ....

....

ii) Stem ....

....

iii) Roots ....

....

Adaptations

Q3 Complete the passage using some of the words from the list below.

temperature salinity extremophobes pressure light levels extremophiles

Microorganisms that have adapted to live in extreme conditions are known as .... For example, bacteria living on deep-sea volcanic vents can cope with very high .... and ....

Q4 Some plants and animals are adapted to **avoid being eaten**.

a) **i)** The fox on the right lives in the Arctic. State **one** feature of the fox that helps it to avoid predators.

....

ii) Explain how the feature described in **i)** helps the fox to avoid predators.

....

b) Wasps are brightly coloured. Explain how this helps protect them against predators.

....

c) State a feature of another organism that helps it to avoid being eaten.

....

Q5 Hayley measured some cubes to find out their surface area to volume ratio. Her results are shown in the table.

Length of cube side (cm)	Surface area of cube (cm^2)	Volume of cube (cm^3)	Surface area: volume ratio
2	24	8	3:1
4	96	64	
6	216	216	
8	384	512	
10	600	1000	

a) Calculate the **surface area : volume ratio** for each cube and write your answers in the table.

Just divide the surface area by the volume.

b) As the cube size becomes larger, what happens to the value of the **surface area : volume ratio**?

....

c) Would you expect the smallest cube (length 2 cm) or the largest cube (length 10 cm) to lose heat more quickly? Explain your answer.

....

d) Use your answers above to explain why a mouse has a thick covering of fur.

....

....

Competition and Environmental Change

Q1 The resources below are **essential** for life.

Light

Plants

Water

Minerals from the soil

Animals

Food

Space

Mates

a) Draw lines to connect the boxes to show which resources are essential for plants, essential for animals and essential for both.

b) What would happen if two species in a habitat need the same resource?

....

c) Give one way that organisms are dependent on other species for their survival.

....

Q2 **Algae** are tiny organisms that are eaten by **fish**. The graph shows how the size of a population of algae in a pond varied throughout one year.

Algae population size

Jan Feb Mar Apr May Jun Jul Aug Sep Oct Nov Dec

Time (months)

a) Suggest two conditions that may have changed in the pond to give more algae in April than in January.

....

b) The number of **fish** in the pond increased rapidly during one month of the year. Suggest which month this was. Explain your answer.

....

....

....

Top Tips: If there's a change in the size or distribution of a population, use information you're given plus your own knowledge to work out the living or non-living factors that might have caused it.

Competition and Environmental Change

Q3 The table shows how the UK's barn owl population has changed over a period of 20 years.

Year	No. of barn owl pairs (thousands)
1970	7
1980	4.5
1990	1.7

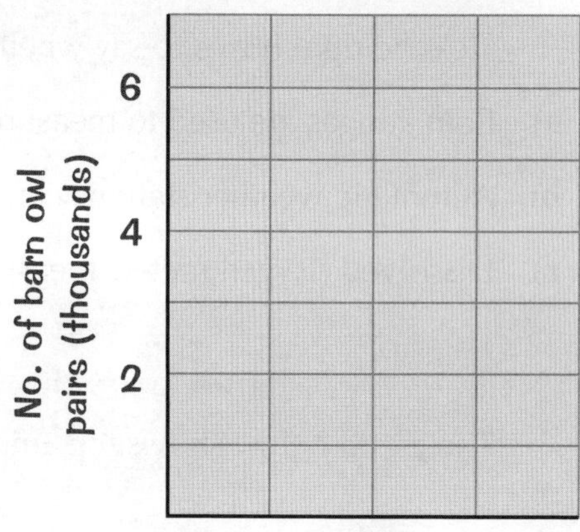

a) Use the table to plot a line graph showing the change in the size of the barn owl population over time. Use the grid provided.

b) Estimate the population size in 1985. ....

c) Suggest **two** reasons why the barn owl population has decreased in recent years.

....

....

Q4 The graph shows the **maximum height** up a mountain at which a **snail** species was found between 1916 and 2008.

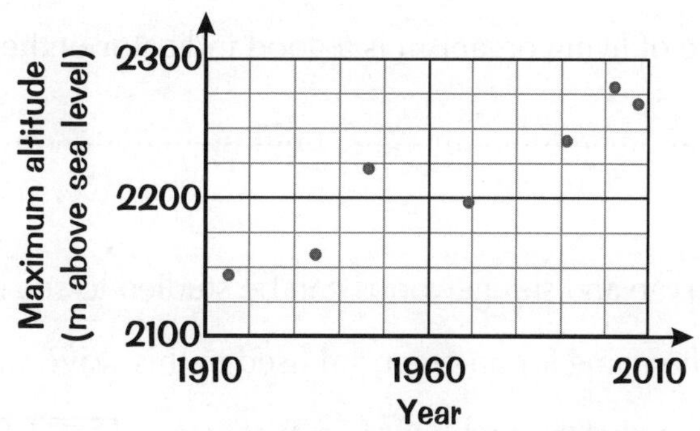

a) From the graph, briefly describe the change in the distribution of the snail species over the last 100 years.

....

b) The **average temperature** on the mountain has **increased** during the last 100 years. Use this information to explain how the change in temperature has affected the distribution of the snail species.

....

....

c) Other than temperature, give an example of a non-living factor that can affect the distribution of a species.

....

Measuring Environmental Change

Q1 Tick the right boxes to say whether the sentences below are **true** or **false**.

		True	False
a)	Rain gauges are used to measure the amount of rainfall in an area.	☐	☐
b)	Automatic weather stations can be used to measure atmospheric temperature.	☐	☐
c)	Dissolved oxygen meters measure the concentration of dissolved carbon in water.	☐	☐

Q2 The graph below shows the amount of sulfur dioxide released in the UK between 1970 and 2003.

a) In which year shown on the graph were sulfur dioxide emissions highest? ....

b) Approximately how much sulfur dioxide was emitted in 2003? ....

c) What type of living organism is a good indicator of the concentration of sulfur dioxide in the air?

....

Q3 Mayfly larvae and sludgeworms can be studied to see how much **sewage** is in water.

a) What is the name for an organism used in this way? ....

Juanita recorded the number of each species in water samples taken at three different distances away from a sewage outlet. Her results are shown on the right.

Distance (km)	No. of mayfly larvae	No. of sludgeworms
1	3	20
2	11	14
3	23	7

b) Give one thing that she would have to do to make this experiment a fair test.

....

c) What can you conclude about the two organisms from these results?

....

....

d) Suggest why sewage may decrease the number of mayfly larvae.

....

....

Pyramids of Biomass

Q1 The **pyramid of biomass** below describes a seashore food chain.

a) Which organism is the producer?

....

b) Which organism is the primary consumer?

....

c) Which trophic level has the greatest biomass?

....

Q2 A single **robin** has a mass of 15 g and eats caterpillars. Each robin eats 25 **caterpillars** that each have a mass of 2 g. The caterpillars feed on 10 **stinging nettles** that together have a mass of 500 g. Study the pyramid diagrams shown then answer the questions that follow.

a) Which is most likely to represent a pyramid of **biomass** for these organisms? ....

b) Explain how you decided on your answer to part **a)** above.

....

c) The stinging nettles are the first trophic level. Where does their energy initially come from?

....

Q3 In the 1950s a chemical called **DDT** was used to control animal pests. DDT was later discovered to be toxic and was detected at very high levels in organisms across food chains, as shown below.

a) Describe what happens to the level of DDT found in organisms as you go up the trophic levels.

....

....

b) Work out by how many times (e.g. 2 times or 70 times) the level of DDT has risen in the following:

i) in the top consumer compared with the producer ....

ii) in the secondary consumer compared with the producer ....

c) Suggest why a pyramid of biomass is a suitable diagram for displaying the problem with DDT.

....

Top Tips: Pyramids of biomass should be drawn to scale, and will almost always end up pyramid-shaped with the producers having the greatest biomass.

Energy Transfer and Decay

Q1 Indicate whether these statements are **true** or **false**.

		True	False
a)	Without sunlight, nearly all life on Earth would die.	☐	☐
b)	Food chains generally have no more than five steps.	☐	☐
c)	Materials are not lost from food chains — they are recycled.	☐	☐
d)	Elements like carbon are passed along food chains.	☐	☐
e)	Energy only is passed between the steps of food chains.	☐	☐
f)	Food chains that include animals with constant body temperatures are less likely to lose energy as heat.	☐	☐

Q2 Look at the picture of the **compost bin** below. Then choose **three** of the features shown and explain how each feature aids the process of decomposition.

decomposers
open top
shredded waste
mesh sides
base in contact with soil

Feature	How it aids decomposition

Q3 Complete the sentences below by circling the correct words.

a) Nearly all life on Earth depends on **food** / **energy** from the Sun.

b) **Plants** / **Animals** can make their own food by a process called **photosynthesis** / **respiration**.

c) To obtain energy animals must **decay** / **eat** plant material or other animals.

d) Animals and plants release energy through the process of **photosynthesis** / **respiration**.

e) Some of the energy obtained by animals is **gained** / **lost** through **growth** / **movement** before it reaches organisms at later steps of the food chain.

f) Some energy is lost between steps of a food chain because it's used to make **edible** / **inedible** materials such as **hair** / **flesh**.

Q4 The sentences below describe how **elements** are **recycled** in a food chain. Sort them into the correct order by numbering them 1 to 6. The first one has been done for you.

☐ Energy released in respiration is lost by decay, heat and movement and the production of waste.

☐ Materials are recycled and returned to the soil by decay.

1 Plants take up minerals from the soil.

☐ Plants use minerals and the products of photosynthesis to make complex nutrients.

☐ Nutrients in plants are passed to animals through feeding and used in respiration to provide energy.

☐ Waste and dead tissues are decayed by microorganisms.

Energy Transfer and Decay

Q5 Living things are made from materials that they take from the world around them.

a) i) Name four **elements** that living organisms contain

....

ii) Where do organisms get these elements?

....

b) Explain how the elements inside organisms are returned to the environment.

....

....

Q6 In a **stable community**, the materials that are taken out of the soil and used are balanced by those that are put back in. Decide whether each of the following examples describes a stable community or not — write **stable** or **not stable** in the spaces provided.

a) A farmer plants a field of wheat. In Autumn he harvests the crop. ....

b) In Autumn leaves fall from trees to the grass below where they decay. ....

c) James rakes up the leaves on the ground of his orchard. ....

d) When Julie mows the lawn she leaves the cuttings on the lawn's surface. ....

Q7 Study the diagram of **energy transfer** shown.

a) Using the figures shown on the diagram, work out the percentage of the Sun's energy that is available in the grass.

....

b) The efficiency of energy transfer from the grass to the next trophic level is 10%. Work out how much energy is available in animal A.

Remember, animal A isn't the only animal at the next level.

....

c) **B** and **C** are processes that represent energy loss. Suggest what these processes might be.

....

d) Why do food chains rarely have more than five trophic levels?

....

....

The Carbon Cycle

Q1 Complete the passage by inserting the most appropriate words from the list below.

respiration **carbohydrates** **microorganisms** **carbon dioxide** **detritus** **photosynthesis** **eating** **waste**

Green plants and algae remove .... from the air and use it in ....
At night plants return this gas to the air through ...., a process that occurs at all times in living organisms including animals and .... Animals obtain a supply of carbon by .... plants. Through digestion, carbon is made available from fats, proteins and .... that are stored in plant tissues. Carbon is released from dead tissues and animal .... by .... feeders.

Q2 Draw lines to match the statements below with their correct endings.

Plants use...	carbon by photosynthesis.
Microorganisms release...	carbon dioxide by decaying waste and dead tissue.
Animals and plants release...	carbon through feeding.
Animals take in...	carbon dioxide to build complex molecules.
Plants take in...	carbon dioxide through respiration.

Q3 The diagram below shows a version of the **carbon cycle**.

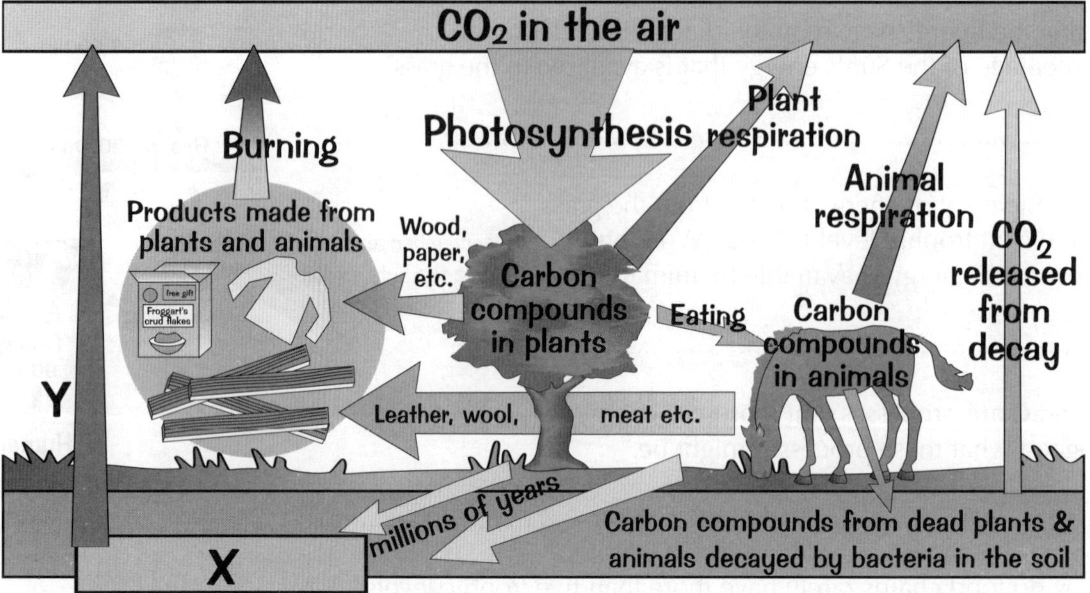

a) Name substance **X** shown on the diagram above. ....

b) Name the process labelled **Y** on the diagram above. ....

Variation

Q1 Complete this passage by circling the **best** word or phrase from each highlighted pair.

Usually, organisms of the same species **have differences / are identical**.

This is partly because different organisms have different **genes / cells**, which are passed on in **gametes / body cells** from which the offspring develop. **Siblings / Identical twins** are exceptions to this. But even these usually have some different features, such as **hair style / eye colour**, and that is due to their **diet / environment**. The differences between individual organisms are known as **variation / inheritance**.

Q2 Helen and Stephanie are identical twins. Helen has dark hair and Stephanie is blonde.

a) Do you think that these are Helen and Stephanie's natural hair colours? Explain your answer.

....

....

b) Helen weighs 7 kg more than Stephanie. Say whether this is due to genes, environment or both, and explain your answer.

....

....

c) Stephanie has a birthmark on her shoulder shaped like a monkey. Helen doesn't.
Do you think birthmarks are caused by your genes? Explain why.

....

....

Q3 Mr O'Riley breeds racehorses. He breeds his best black racing stallion, Snowball, with his best black racing mare, Goldie.

a) Why is there no guarantee that any foal born will be a champion racer?

....

....

b) Will the colour of the newborn foal be due to genes or to environment?

....

Top Tips: Features controlled by genes (e.g. hair colour) can be passed on to an organism's offspring — but features controlled by the environment (e.g. hair style) normally can't be passed on.

Variation

Q4 The peppered moth is an insect that is often found on tree bark and is preyed on by birds. There are two varieties of peppered moth — a light form and a dark form. Until the 1850s, the light form was more common, but after then the dark form increased a lot, particularly near cities.

Moths on tree bark in unpolluted area

Moths on tree bark in polluted area

a) Why do you think the lighter variety of the peppered moth was more common originally?

Hint: Use the diagrams to help you.

....

....

b) In the 1850s, the Industrial Revolution began — there was rapid growth in heavy industries in Britain. Why do you think the number of dark moths increased after this time?

....

....

c) Do you think a difference in genes or in environment would cause a dark moth to suddenly appear in a population of light moths? ....

Q5 Nazneen grows three strawberry plants and three sunflowers.

a) Why do the strawberry plants look so different to the sunflower plants?

....

b) Sunflower plants reproduce by sexual reproduction. Why could Nazneen not expect her three sunflower plants to be exactly the same height?

Sexual reproduction is where two gametes fuse together.

....

....

c) Nazneen's strawberry plants were grown by asexual reproduction so they have identical genes. However, her strawberry plants are not all exactly the same height. Explain why this might be.

....

....

Genes, Chromosomes and DNA

Q1 Complete the passage using some of the words given below.

DNA	nucleus	genes	chromosomes	membrane	allele

Most cells in your body contain a structure called the ....

This structure contains strands of genetic information, packaged into ....

These strands are made of a chemical called ....

Sections of genetic material that control different characteristics are called ....

Q2 Write out these structures in order of size, **starting with the smallest**.

nucleus	gene	chromosome	cell

1. .... 2. .... 3. .... 4. ....

Q3 Which of the following is the correct definition of the term '**alleles**'? Underline your choice.

'Alleles' is the collective term for all the genes found on a pair of chromosomes.

'Alleles' are different forms of the same gene.

'Alleles' are identical organisms produced by asexual reproduction.

Q4 Only one of the following statements is true. Tick the correct one.

There are two chromosome 7s in a human nucleus, both from the person's mother. ☐

There are two chromosome 7s in a human nucleus, both from the person's father. ☐

There are two chromosome 7s in a human nucleus, one from each parent. ☐

There is only one chromosome 7 in a human nucleus. ☐

Q5 The human chromosome 15 contains a gene that is involved in controlling eye colour. How many chromosome 15s would you expect to find in each of the following cells?

a) A cell in the retina of the eye. ....

b) A muscle cell. ....

c) A sperm cell. ....

Top Tips: As well as needing to know where chromosomes and genes are found, you also need to know that genes determine an organism's characteristics by controlling how they develop.

Reproduction

Q1 Circle the correct words in each statement below to complete the sentences.

a) Sexual reproduction involves **one** / **two** individual(s).

b) The cells that are involved in sexual reproduction are called **parent cells** / **gametes**.

c) Asexual reproduction produces offspring with **identical** / **different** genes to the parent.

d) In sexual reproduction the sperm cell contains **the same number of** / **half as many** chromosomes as the **fertilised** egg.

e) **Asexual** / **Sexual** reproduction creates offspring with different characteristics to the parent(s).

Q2 Complete the following sentences.

Billy...?

a) Offspring that are identical to their parent are called ....

b) The human male gamete is a ....

c) The process that occurs when two gametes fuse is ....

Q3 Lucy cut her hand, but a week later she noticed that the cut had almost disappeared. The skin covering it looked just the same as the skin on the rest of her hand. This happened by the same process as **asexual reproduction**.

a) Where did the new skin cells on Lucy's hand come from?

....

....

b) Suggest why the skin on Lucy's hand looked the same as it had before she had cut herself.

....

....

c) Suggest why it took a week for the cut to heal.

....

....

Q4 Explain how a human baby receives genes from both its father and its mother, but still only has 46 chromosomes in its cells.

....

....

....

Cloning

Q1 Plants can be cloned from **cuttings**, as shown in the diagram below.

Draw a line from each description below to its correct place on the diagram.

The cuttings are kept in moist conditions until they are ready to plant.	Cloned plant	Cuttings are taken, each with a new bud on	Parent plant

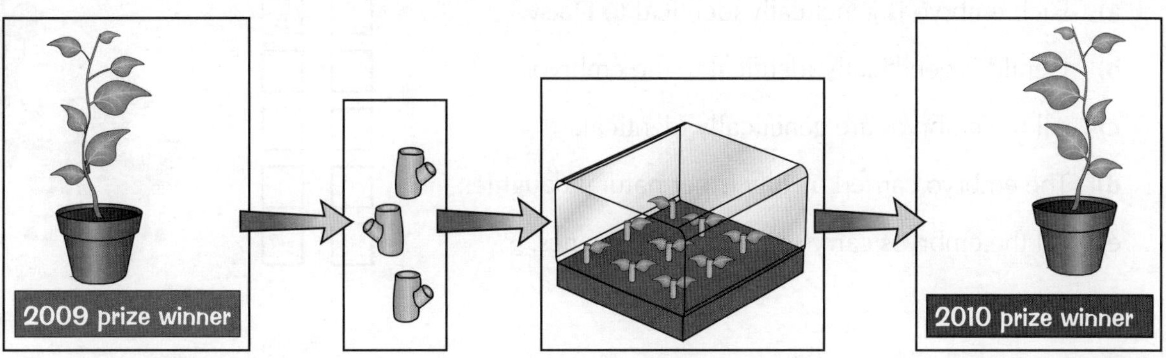

Q2 Plants can also be cloned using **tissue culture**.

a) Briefly describe how tissue culture works.

....

....

b) Give **two** advantages of cloning plants using tissue culture.

Advantage 1: ....

Advantage 2: ....

Q3 **Dolly** the sheep was cloned from an adult cell.

Write the correct letter (A, B, C or D) next to each label below to show where it belongs on the diagram.

removing and discarding a nucleus ....

implantation in a surrogate mother ....

useful nucleus extracted ....

formation of a diploid cell ....

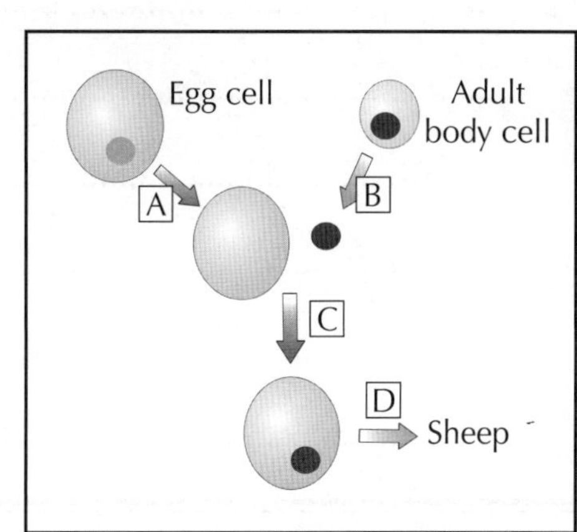

Cloning

Q4 Read the passage before deciding whether the statements that follow are **true** or **false**.

> Sperm was collected from Gerald the stallion and used to artificially inseminate Daisy the mare. An embryo was then removed from Daisy and divided into separate cells, each of which was allowed to grow into a new embryo. These new embryos were then implanted into other horses, including Rosie, Ruby and Jilly.

		True	False
a)	Each embryo is genetically identical to Daisy.	☐	☐
b)	Gerald is genetically identical to the embryos.	☐	☐
c)	All the embryos are genetically identical.	☐	☐
d)	The embryo carried by Jilly is her natural daughter.	☐	☐
e)	All the embryos carry some of Daisy's genes.	☐	☐

Q5 Complete the passage below choosing from the words provided.

nucleus growth dividing physically genetically host egg donor electric shock

Clones are .... identical organisms. They can be made by scientists in the laboratory by removing the .... from an .... cell.

It is replaced with a nucleus taken from an adult .... cell.

The cell is then stimulated by an .... to start ....

The embryo that results from this is .... identical to the .... cell.

Q6 Summarise the **issues** involved in cloning.

....

....

....

....

....

....

Top Tips: As well as the ethical issues involved in cloning, you also need to know about the economic issues — why it's useful and can do things that would be expensive by other methods.

Genetic Engineering

Q1 Read the article below about **GM crops** and answer the questions that follow.

There are many reasons for genetically modifying crops. Two important reasons are to make them pest-resistant and to make them resistant to herbicides (weedkillers).

At the moment no one's growing any GM crops commercially in the UK. Recently, though, some farmers took part in crop trials set up by the Government, to see what effects growing herbicide-tolerant GM crops might have on wildlife. There were four kinds of crops in the trials — beet, spring oilseed rape, maize and winter oilseed rape.

Fields of various sizes were chosen for the study. In each case, the farmer split one of their normal fields in half. They then grew a 'normal' crop in one half and its GM equivalent in the other. Apart from that, they did everything normally — ploughing the field, adding fertiliser etc. in the same way as they usually would. The only difference was with herbicides — with the GM crops, the farmers followed instructions about how much of which herbicides to use, and when to apply them. They applied herbicides to the 'normal' crop as they usually would.

As the crops grew, the government researchers counted the number of weeds growing, and the number of weed seeds produced in each half of the field. They also monitored the populations of insects, slugs, spiders and other wildlife.

The researchers found that with three crops (beet, spring oilseed rape and winter oilseed rape), growing normal crops was better for wildlife — they found more butterflies and bees on the normal crops. They also found more flowering weeds (the kinds that butterflies and bees prefer) on the side with the normal crops. With maize, oddly, the opposite seemed to be true — there were more weeds, and more butterflies and bees, around the GM crops.

a) Explain the **purpose** of the trial described in the article.

....

....

b) **i)** Suggest why each field was divided in half rather than choosing separate fields for normal and GM crops.

....

....

Farmer Gideon had a brand new combine harvester and he wasn't going to give anyone the keys.

ii) Give two things that were done in the same way by the farmers for the GM crops and for the normal crops. Suggest why these things were kept constant.

....

....

iii) Give one thing that was done differently for the GM crops and for the normal crops. Suggest why this was not kept constant for both types of crop.

....

....

Genetic Engineering

c) Herbicides were used on **both** the normal and the GM crops in this trial.

i) Explain why fewer weeds normally grow among herbicide-resistant crops.

....

....

ii) Explain how growing herbicide-resistant crops in the UK could benefit:

farmers. ....

....

shoppers buying these products. ....

....

d) The result for the **maize** crop was surprising. Tick the box next to the **correct** statement below.

☐ The result was surprising because wildlife preferred the GM maize even though there were fewer weeds.

☐ The result was surprising because there were more weeds with the GM crop even though more herbicide was used.

☐ The result was surprising because bees and butterflies are usually repelled by GM crops.

e) Some people are **worried** that growing GM crops will lead to a reduction in **biodiversity**.

i) Do you think that the results of this trial support the above fear? Explain your answer.

....

....

ii) Give two other reasons why people are concerned about GM crops.

....

....

iii) Suggest one possible reason for the unusual result seen with the maize crop in this trial.

....

....

Evolution

Q1 Put crosses in the right columns to say which characteristics refer to which **group of organisms**.

	Plant	Animal
Travels to new places		
Makes its own food		
Is fixed to the ground		
May be single celled		

Q2 The diagram below shows the **evolutionary relationships** of four different species.

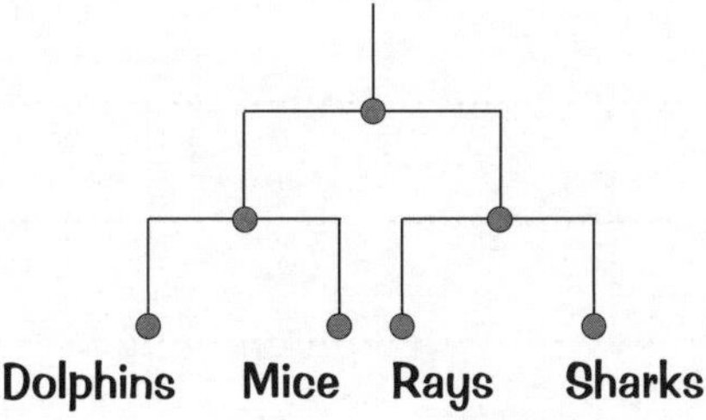

a) Tick the box next to the pair of species below that has the most recent common ancestor.

- [ ] Mice and Rays.
- [ ] Rays and Sharks.
- [ ] Mice and Sharks.

b) Sharks and dolphins share similar characteristics even though they are not closely related. Suggest **one** thing this could tell us about their ecological relationship.

....

Q3 The theory of evolution by **natural selection** was developed by Charles Darwin. Tick the sentences below that describe aspects of natural selection correctly.

- [ ] There is variation within species caused by differences in their genes.
- [ ] Genes don't vary enough within species to make members of the same species look different.
- [ ] The best adapted animals and plants are most likely to survive.
- [ ] Some characteristics are passed on through reproduction from parent to offspring.
- [ ] Animals that have successfully adapted do not need to produce offspring.

Evolution

Q4 The buff tip moth's appearance **mimics a broken stick**, making it well-camouflaged. The statements below describe how this feature might have evolved. Write numbers in the boxes to show the order the statements should be in.

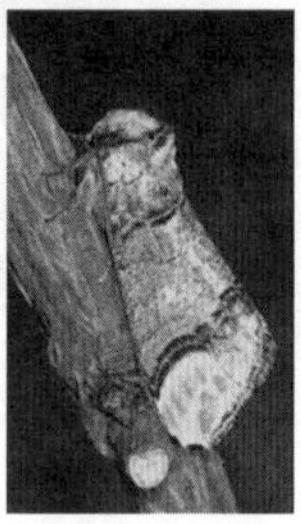

- ☐ Ancestors to the buff tip moth showed variation in their appearance. Some had genes that made them look a bit like a stick.
- ☐ So the stick-like moths were more likely to survive and reproduce.
- ☐ Genes that made the moths look like sticks were more likely to be passed on to the next generation.
- ☐ Short-sighted birds in poor light didn't spot the stick-like moths.

Q5 A and B are fossilised bones from the legs of **ancestors** of the **modern horse**. Some scientists believe that animals with legs like fossil A gradually developed into animals with legs like fossil B.

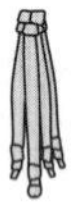

A

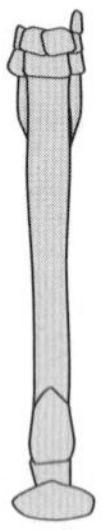

B

a) Suggest **two** reasons why this change may have happened.

....

....

....

....

b) Read the passage below.

> It is thought that there was a stage in the development of the horse between A and B, during which the leg bone would have looked like C.
> Animals with legs like fossil D are closely related to animals with legs like fossil B.
> However, those animals with legs like fossil D aren't direct ancestors of the modern horse.

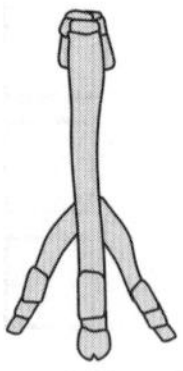

C  D

Use all the information in this question to label the evolutionary tree below with the letters A-D.

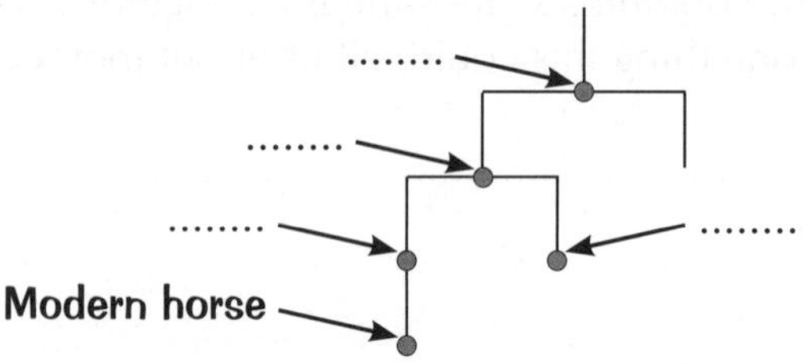

....

....

....

Modern horse

Q6 A student incubated a sample of bacteria on an agar plate. The bacteria multiplied to form a plaque. He then added an **antibiotic** to the bacteria. Most of the bacteria died. He incubated the plate again and the remaining bacteria reproduced to form a new plaque. He added the **same** antibiotic to the bacterial plaque and **none of the bacteria died**. Explain these results.

....

....

More About Evolution

Q1 Which of the statements below gives a reason why some scientists did **not** at first agree with Darwin's idea of **natural selection**? Circle the letters next to the correct statements.

A He could not explain how characteristics could be inherited.

B Characteristics that are caused by the environment can be inherited.

C They thought he was making up the evidence.

D They felt that Darwin was influenced by religious rather than scientific ideas.

E There wasn't enough evidence to convince many scientists.

F They didn't trust men with beards.

Q2 Complete this passage by circling the **best** word or phrase from each highlighted pair.

Bismarck / Lamarck argued that if a characteristic was used a lot by an organism then it would become **more developed / stunted** during its lifetime. For example if an anteater used its tongue a lot to reach ants in anthills, its tongue would get **longer / shorter**. He believed this acquired characteristic would be passed on to **the next generation / animals living nearby**.

Q3 More than one hypothesis has been suggested to explain how evolution occurs.

Tick the boxes by the pieces of evidence below that **do not support** Lamarck's hypothesis:

- ☐ Kestrels have good eyesight to help them to spot mice from far away.
- ☐ People with dyed blue hair do not have children with blue hair.
- ☐ Hummingbirds have long tongues that enable them to feed on nectar from long flowers.
- ☐ Sheep whose tails are cut short give birth to lambs with full-length tails.

Q4 Lamarck and Darwin came up with **different ideas** to explain how evolution works.

Give **two** reasons why scientists may come up with different ideas to explain similar observations.

....

....

Top Tips: Scientists often come up with different hypotheses to explain their observations. The only way to find out which is right is to find evidence to support or disprove each one.

Mixed Questions — Biology 1b

Q1 The graph shows how the **body temperatures** of a camel and a goat change throughout the day in a hot desert.

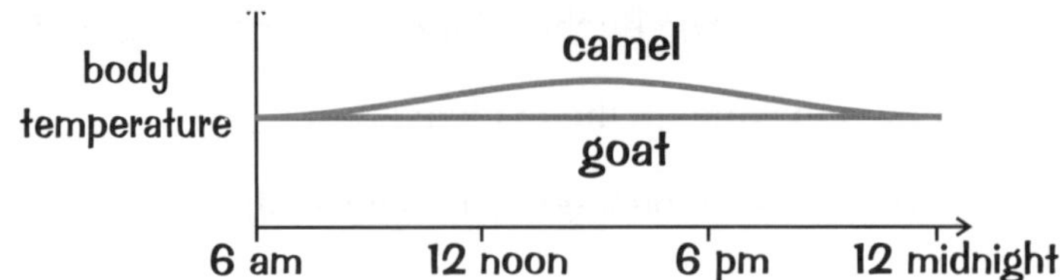

a) Between 6 am and 12 noon, what happened to the body temperature:

i) of the camel? ....

ii) of the goat? ....

b) Which one of the animals keeps cool by sweating? ....

c) Explain why animals that use sweating to keep cool can't survive well in deserts.

....

d) Camels have evolved to tolerate changes in body temperature. State the name of Darwin's theory of how evolution occurs.

....

Q2 The normal numbers of **chromosomes** in the body cells of some different species are:

donkeys — 31 pairs of chromosomes	**horses — 32 pairs of chromosomes**
lions — 19 pairs of chromosomes	**tigers — 19 pairs of chromosomes**

Mating between different, closely-related species occasionally results in offspring. However, the offspring are usually **sterile**. For example, a **mule** is a cross between a donkey and a horse, and a **liger** is a cross between a lion and a tiger.

a) Use the information above to work out the number of chromosomes in the body cells of a mule.

Hint: Think about the number of chromosomes in the gametes of donkeys and horses.

....

....

b) Mules are almost always sterile, but ligers can occasionally produce offspring of their own. Explain this by considering the number of chromosomes of ligers and mules.

....

....

Mixed Questions — Biology 1b

Q3 An experiment was done with two **fertilised natterjack toad eggs**. The eggs came from completely different parents. The nucleus of **egg A** was put into **egg B**, and the nucleus of egg B was **removed** (see the diagram on the right).

a) Egg **B** grew into a toad. Would you expect it to look more like the parents of egg **A** or the parents of egg **B**? Explain your answer.

....

b) The technique used to create Dolly the sheep also involved removing genetic material from an egg cell. However, Dolly was a **clone**, whereas the toad produced in this experiment was not. Explain why this is.

....

....

c) **Competition** with other amphibians has had an effect on the number of natterjack toads. Suggest **two** things that the toads may have been competing for.

....

d) Because of their permeable skin, amphibians are '**indicator species**'.

Explain what this term means. ....

....

Q4 Scientists tried to **genetically modify** some bacteria. They inserted a piece of DNA containing both the human gene for **growth hormone** and a gene for **penicillin resistance** into a bacterium. Afterwards, the bacteria were grown on agar plates containing penicillin.

a) Why were the bacteria grown on plates containing penicillin?

Hint: It's hard to tell by looking if the growth hormone gene has been inserted correctly.

....

....

b) Give **one advantage** of producing growth hormone with bacteria, rather than by other methods.

....

c) The bacteria produced were all genetically identical.
What type of reproduction do you think took place?

....

Mixed Questions — Biology 1b

Q5 The diagram below shows a **food chain** observed on the savannahs of Tanzania. It also shows the amount of **energy** available in each trophic level.

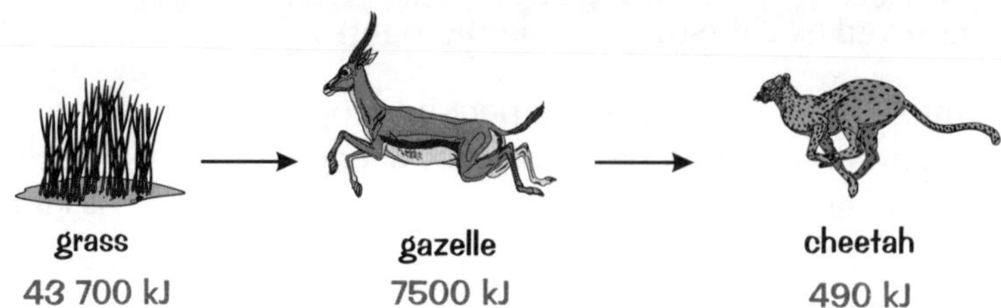

a) **i)** How much energy is lost from the 1st trophic level (grass) to the next (gazelle)?

....

ii) Calculate the percentage of energy in the grass that is transferred to the gazelle.

....

b) Suggest two ways in which energy might be lost by the gazelle.

....

....

c) **Carbon** also moves through the food chain. It is continuously being **recycled** from one form to another as the diagram below shows.

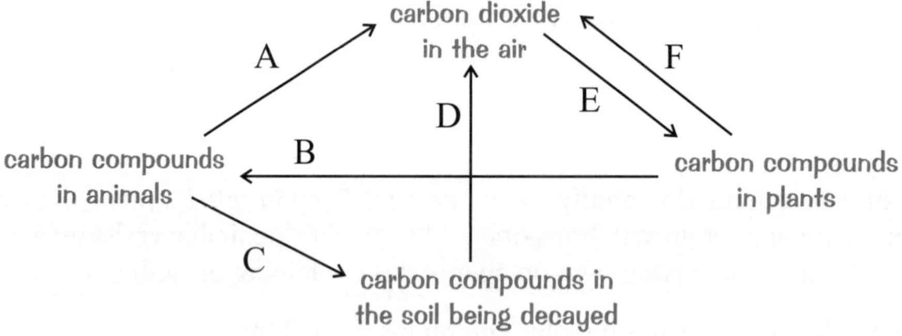

Name the processes labelled **A**, **B**, **C**, **D**, **E** and **F** in the diagram.

A .... **B** ....

C .... **D** ....

E .... **F** ....

d) Cheetahs don't always eat all of the meat on a gazelle. What is not eaten begins to **decompose**. The savannahs are warm and open (giving a good supply of air). Explain how these conditions will influence the rate at which the meat decomposes.

....

....

Cells

Q1 Plant and animal cells have **similarities** and **differences**.
Complete each statement below by choosing the correct words.

a) **Plant** / **animal** cells, but not **plant** / **animal** cells, contain chloroplasts.

b) Plant cells and algal cells have a **vacuole** / **cell wall**, which is made of cellulose.

c) **Both plant and animal cells** / **only animal cells** contain ribosomes, which is where **carbohydrates** / **proteins** are made in the cell.

d) The cell **wall** / **membrane** holds the cell together and controls what goes in and out.

Q2 State what the following cell structures **contain** or are **made of** and what their **functions** are.

a) The **nucleus** contains ....

Its function is ....

b) **Chloroplasts** contain ....

Their function is ....

c) The **cell wall** is made of ....

Its function is ....

Q3 **Mitochondria** are very important cellular structures.

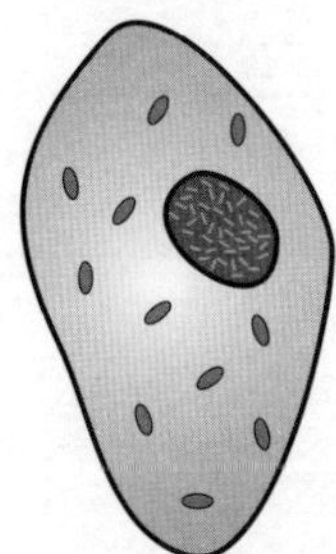

a) Is this cell an animal or plant cell? ....

b) Draw an arrow pointing to one of the mitochondria in the cell.

c) Why are mitochondria so important?

....

....

Q4 Label the diagrams of the **yeast cell** and **bacterial cell** below.

d) Explain why the diagram on the right must be the bacterial cell and not the yeast cell.

....

Diffusion

Q1 Complete the passage below by choosing the most appropriate words.

Diffusion is the **direct** / **random** movement of particles from an area where they are at a **higher** / **lower** concentration to an area where they are at a **higher** / **lower** concentration. There is a **net** / **rod** movement of particles from that area. The rate of diffusion is faster when the concentration gradient is **bigger** / **smaller** and in **liquids** / **gases**.

Q2 The first diagram below shows a **cup of water** which has just had a **drop of dye** added.

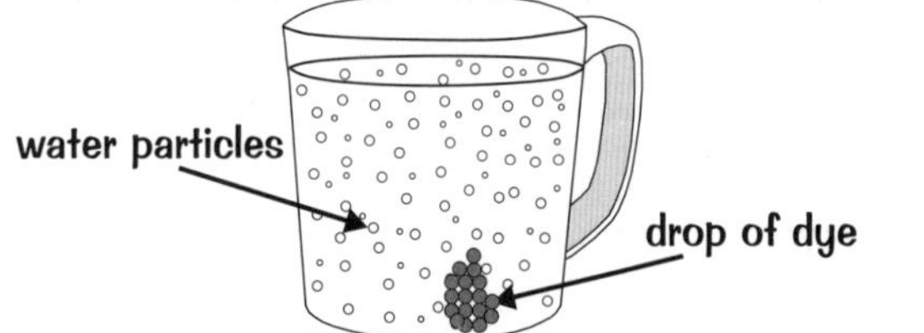

a) In the second cup above, draw the molecules of **dye** in the water after an hour.

b) Predict how the rate of diffusion of the dye would change if a large drop of dye is used rather than a small drop of dye.

....

c) Explain the movement of the dye particles in terms of differences in concentration.

....

....

Q3 Patsy was studying in her bedroom. Her dad was cooking curry for tea in the kitchen. Soon Patsy could smell the curry that her dad was making.

a) Her dad was warm so he switched on a fan. Suggest what effect the fan would have on the rate that the curry particles spread through the house.

....

b) After tasting the curry, Patsy's dad added more curry powder. What effect would this have on the smell of the curry? Explain your answer using the word **concentration**.

....

....

....

Diffusion

Q4 Some statements about **diffusion** are written below.
Decide which are correct and then write **true** or **false** in the spaces.

a) Diffusion takes place in all types of substances. ....

b) Diffusion is usually quicker in liquids than in gases. ....

c) Diffusion happens more quickly when there is a higher concentration gradient. ....

d) Dissolved substances can move in and out of cells by diffusion. ....

e) Oxygen molecules are too large to diffuse through cell membranes. ....

Q5 Two models of diffusion are shown below.

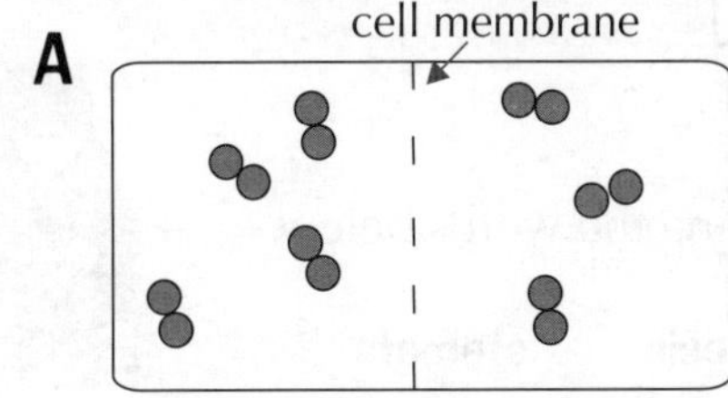

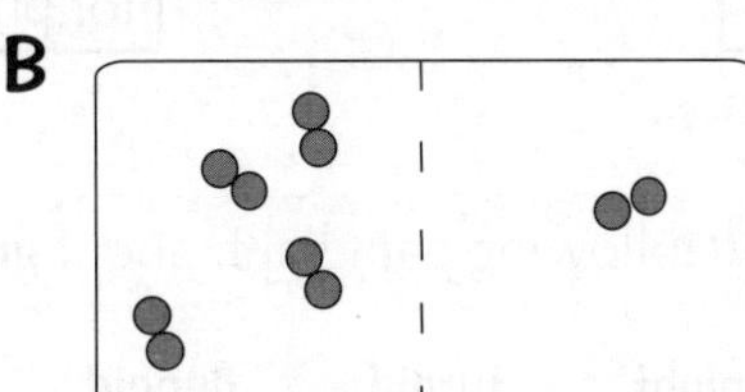

a) Would you expect the molecules to diffuse **faster** in situation A or B? ....

b) Explain your answer.

....

Q6 Phil was investigating the diffusion of **glucose** and **starch** through a **membrane**.
He placed equal amounts of glucose solution and starch solution inside a bag designed to act like a cell membrane. He then put the bag into a beaker of water.

a) After 20 minutes, Phil tested the water for the presence of starch and glucose. Circle which of the following you would expect to be found in the water outside the bag:

glucose **starch**

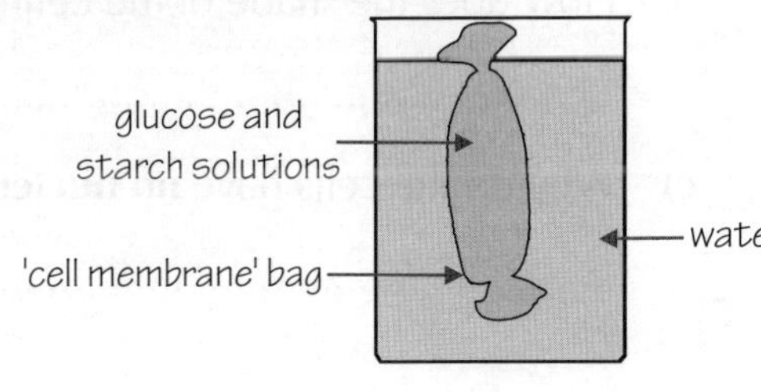

b) Explain your answer to part **a)**.

....

....

....

Top Tips: Don't forget it's only small molecules that can diffuse through cell membranes — amino acids, for example. Big hulking things like proteins are just too darn big to fit through.

Specialised Cells

Q1 Give the correct name for each of the specialised cells described below.

a) These cells transport oxygen around the body. ....

b) The male reproductive cell. ....

c) Cells that open and close stomata on leaves. ....

d) The female reproductive cell. ....

Q2 Below are three features of **palisade leaf cells**. Draw lines to match each feature to its function.

Feature	Function
Lots of chloroplasts	gives a large surface area for absorbing CO_2
Tall shape	means you can pack more cells in at the top of the leaf
Thin shape	for photosynthesis

Q3 Complete the following paragraph about **guard cells**, using the words below.

night **turgid** **flaccid** **photosynthesis** **stomata**

Guard cells open and close the .... When the plant has lots of water the guard cells are .... This makes the stomata open, so gases can be exchanged for .... When the plant is short of water the guard cells become ...., making the stomata close. They also close at .... to save water.

Q4 Red blood cells are adapted to **carry oxygen**.

a) What **shape** are red blood cells? ....

b) How does the shape of the cell help it carry oxygen?

....

c) Why do the cells have **no nucleus**?

....

Q5 Below is a list of features of **reproductive cells**. Decide which ones are found in **sperm** cells and which ones are found in **egg** cells.

	Sperm	Egg
a) A long tail	☐	☐
b) Enzymes to digest cell membranes	☐	☐
c) A large food reserve	☐	☐
d) Lots of mitochondria	☐	☐
e) A streamlined head	☐	☐

Cell Organisation

Q1 Sort the following list by writing each term in the correct place in the table below.

sperm	blood	digestive system	snail
cat	liver	egg (human)	stomach
reproductive system	muscle	eye	dog
excretory system	white blood cell	heart	small intestine

Cell	Tissue	Organ	Organ system	Organism

Q2 Tick the boxes to show whether the following statements are **true** or **false**.

	True	False
a) The liver produces bile.	☐	☐
b) Organisms have only one organ system.	☐	☐
c) Glandular tissue produces substances including enzymes.	☐	☐
d) A heart contains different types of tissue.	☐	☐
e) The inside of the gut is covered by epithelial tissue.	☐	☐
f) An epithelial cell is approximately 0.1 cm long.	☐	☐
g) The stomach is over 1000 times longer than an epithelial cell.	☐	☐

Q3 Put the words below in the correct order to fill in the boxes showing how cells in the digestive system are organised.

stomach

human

epithelial cells

epithelial tissue

↓
↓
↓
digestive system
↓

Cell Organisation

Q4 The **digestive system** is an organ system, made up of tissues and organs.

a) Complete the passage by choosing the most appropriate words from the list below.

muscular tissue	**churn**	**liver**	**nutrients**
bile	**materials**	**organs**	**tissues**

The digestive system exchanges .... with the environment by taking in .... and releasing substances, such as .... The digestive system is made up of ...., like the stomach and the .... The stomach is made up of various different ...., for example ...., which moves the stomach wall to .... up the food.

b) Describe the job of the glandular tissue in the stomach.

....

c) Name **two** glands in the digestive system.

....

Q5 Large multicellular organisms develop **organs systems**. During development, cells **differentiate**.

a) Explain the purpose of organs systems in large multicellular organisms.

....

b) Define the term 'differentiation'.

....

....

Q6 Define the following terms:

a) a tissue

....

b) an organ

....

c) an organ system

....

Plant Structure and Photosynthesis

Q1 **Photosynthesis** is the process that produces 'food' in plants.
Use some of the words below to complete the equation for photosynthesis.

oxygen carbon dioxide nitrogen water glucose sodium chloride

.... + ... $\xrightarrow[\text{chlorophyll}]{\text{sunlight}}$ .... + ...

Q2 Plants are made up of cells, tissues, organs and organs systems.

a) Name **three** organs found in a plant.

....

b) Describe the purpose of each of the tissues below in a plant.

Mesophyll tissue: ....

Epidermal tissue: ....

Xylem and phloem: ....

Q3 The rate of photosynthesis in some pondweed was recorded by counting the bubbles produced per minute at equal intervals during the day.

No. bubbles per minute	Time of day
0	06.00
10	12.00
20	18.00
0	

a) The time for the final reading is missing. Predict what the time is likely to be.

....

b) Explain why the rate of photosynthesis is 0 bubbles per minute for this time of day.

....

c) Suggest where plants get their food from at this time of day.

....

d) Plot a bar graph on the grid on the right to display the results shown on the table.

Don't forget about the scales on your graph.

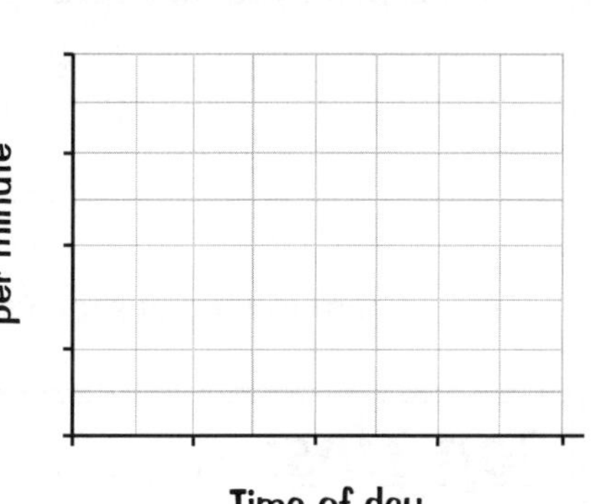

Plant Structure and Photosynthesis

Q4 The graph below shows the **oxygen** and **carbon dioxide** exchanged by a plant. The concentration of each gas was measured next to the leaves as light intensity increased.

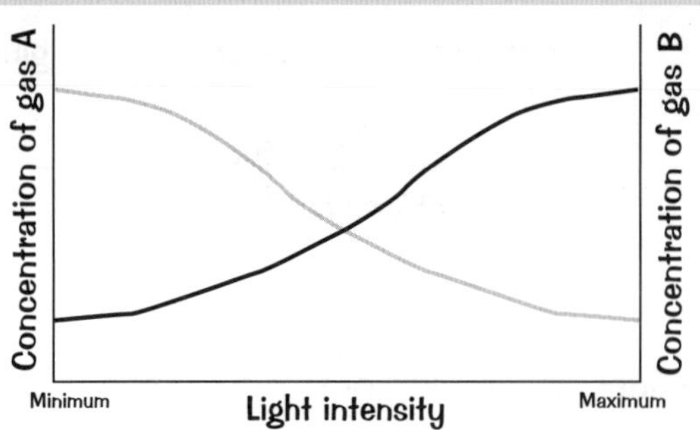

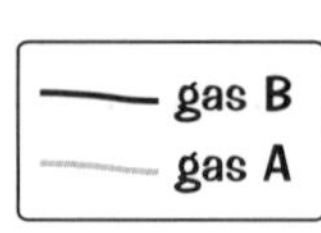

a) i) Which gas is oxygen and which is carbon dioxide?

Gas A is .... Gas B is ....

ii) Explain how you decided.

....

....

b) State the relationships between the following:

i) the light intensity and the concentration of carbon dioxide.

....

ii) the light intensity and the concentration of oxygen.

....

Q5 Jack conducted an experiment to investigate the effect of light on photosynthesis. He placed one plant (plant A) in the **dark** for 24 hours, and another plant (plant B) in bright **sunlight**. Jack tested a leaf from each plant for **starch**.

a) Which plant would you expect to contain more starch?

....

b) Explain your answer to part **a)** above.

....

....

c) Where in the palisade cells of leaves does photosynthesis happen? ....

Top Tips: If you get stuck on a photosynthesis question, jot down the good old equation. You'll see what's needed for photosynthesis and what's produced, which should help you out. Hooray.

The Rate of Photosynthesis

Q1 Below are some straightforward questions about **limiting factors**. Hooray.

a) List **three** factors that can limit the rate of photosynthesis.

....

b) Explain the meaning of the term "limiting factor".

....

c) The limiting factor at a particular time depends on the environmental conditions, e.g. season (such as winter). Name two other environmental conditions that may affect the rate of photosynthesis.

....

Q2 Seth investigated the effect of different concentrations of **carbon dioxide** on the rate of photosynthesis of his Swiss cheese plant. He measured the rate of photosynthesis with increasing light intensity at **three** different CO_2 concentrations. The results are shown on the graph below.

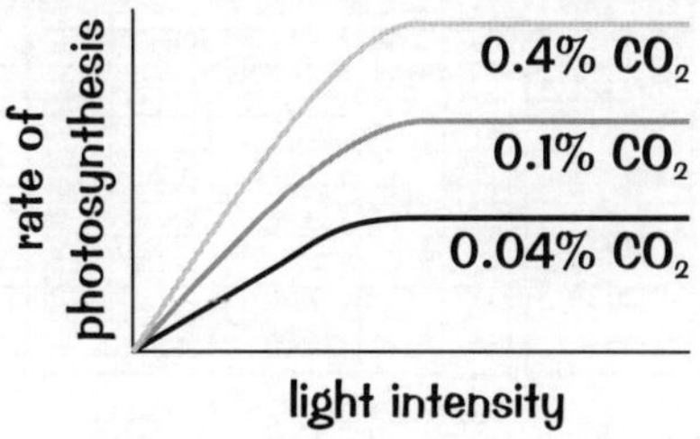

a) What effect does increasing the concentration of CO_2 have on the rate of photosynthesis?

....

....

b) Explain why all the graphs level off eventually.

....

....

Think about the third limiting factor.

Q3 Sunlight contains light of different **wavelengths**, some of which we see as different **colours**. The amount of light absorbed at each wavelength for the green pigment **chlorophyll** is shown below.

a) What wavelengths and colours of light are best absorbed by chlorophyll?

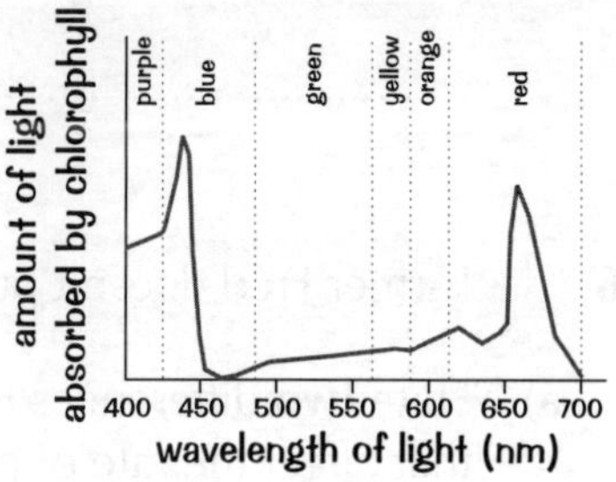

....

b) Suggest how you could use the information on the graph to increase the growth rate of plants in a greenhouse.

....

Q4 Explain why a farmer should ideally have **enough** CO_2 in his greenhouse but **not too much**.

....

....

The Rate of Photosynthesis

Q5 Lucy investigated the **volume of oxygen** produced by pondweed at **different intensities of light**. Her results are shown in the table below.

Relative light intensity	1	2	3	4	5
Volume of oxygen evolved in 10 minutes (ml)	12	25	13	48	61

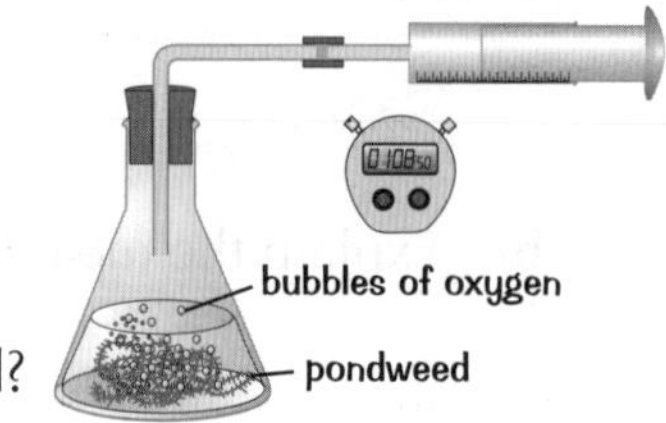

a) What was Lucy measuring by recording the volume of oxygen produced?

....

b) Plot a graph of her results.

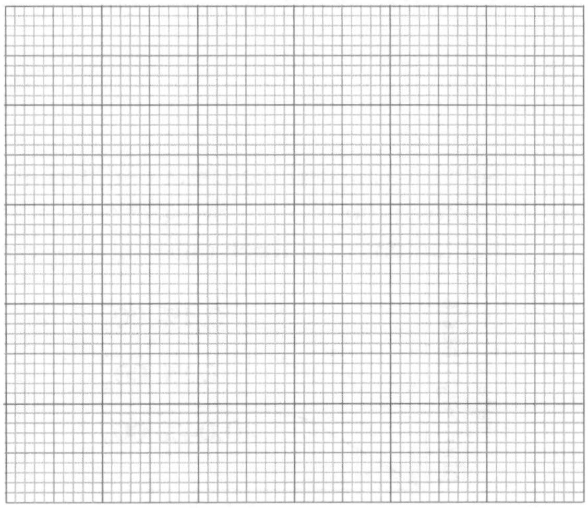

c) i) One of Lucy's results is probably wrong. Circle this point on the graph.

ii) Suggest what error Lucy might have made when she collected this result.

....

....

....

d) Describe the relationship shown on the graph between light intensity and photosynthesis rate.

....

....

e) Would you expect this relationship to continue if Lucy continued to increase the light intensity? Explain your answer.

....

....

Q6 Farmer Fred doesn't put his cows out during the winter because the grass is not growing.

a) State **two** differences between summer and winter conditions that affect the rate of photosynthesis in the grass.

1. ....

2. ....

b) How are the rate of photosynthesis and the growth rate of grass related?

....

....

The Rate of Photosynthesis

Q7 Graham decided to build a **greenhouse** to grow his plants in.

a) List **three** reasons why a greenhouse is an ideal environment for growing plants.

....

....

....

b) i) What could Graham add to his greenhouse in the **winter** for better growth?

....

ii) What should he add in the **summer** to ensure it doesn't get too hot?

....

iii) What addition would be useful at **night** if he wants the plants to continue photosynthesising?

....

iv) Why might it be better to install a **paraffin heater** rather than an electric heater?

....

Q8 Average daytime summer temperatures in different habitats around the world are recorded in the table below.

Habitat	Temperature (°C)
Forest	19
Arctic	0
Desert	32
Grassland	22
Rainforest	27

a) Plot a **bar chart** for these results on the grid.

b) From the values for temperature, in which area would you expect fewest plants to grow?

....

c) Suggest a reason for your answer above using the terms **enzymes** and **photosynthesis**.

....

....

d) **Explain** why very few plants can usually grow in the desert even though it has a much higher average temperature than the rainforest where many varieties of plants can grow.

....

How Plants Use Glucose

Q1 Complete the passage below by choosing the most appropriate words from the list below.

convert **leaves** **margarine** **cells** **cellulose**
cooking oil **energy** **walls** **lipids**

Plants make glucose in their .... Some of it is used for respiration, which releases .... and allows the plant to .... the rest of the glucose into other substances and build new ....

In rapidly growing plants, glucose is converted into .... to build cell .... Seeds can store glucose in the form of ....

For example, we use seeds to make .... and ....

Q2 Plants use glucose to make **protein**. Humans eat plants and animals as sources of protein.

a) What ions do plants need to absorb from the soil in order to produce protein? ....

b) Below is a graph comparing the nutrients in dhal and steak, including their protein content. What percentage of your recommended daily allowance of protein is provided by 100 g of the following?

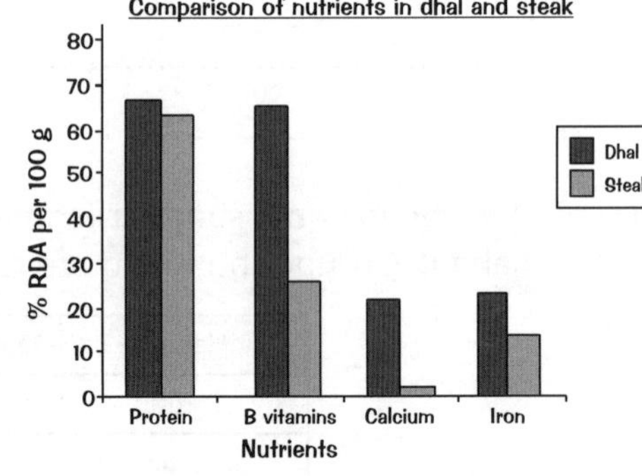

dhal ....

steak ....

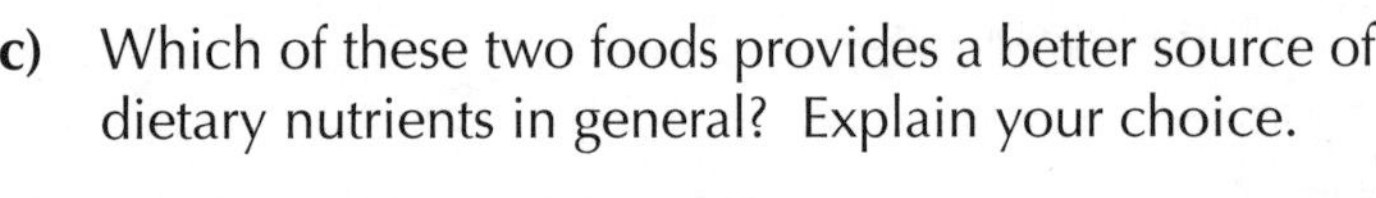

c) Which of these two foods provides a better source of dietary nutrients in general? Explain your choice.

....

....

d) Suggest where the amino acids that make up the protein found in steak originally came from.

....

Q3 New potato plants are grown from potato **tubers**, which are stores of **starch**.

a) Suggest how the new plants obtain the energy needed for growth.

....

b) Explain why the plants no longer need this energy source once they have grown above the soil.

....

c) Why do the tubers store starch, not glucose?

....

Distribution of Organisms

Q1 Tick the boxes to show whether the following statements are **true** or **false**.

		True	False
a)	A habitat is the place where an organism lives.	☐	☐
b)	The distribution of an organism is how an organism interacts with its habitat.	☐	☐
c)	You can use quadrats to study the distribution of an organism.	☐	☐

Q2 Name **three** environmental factors that may affect where an organism is found.

1. ....

2. ....

3. ....

Q3 Dan wanted to investigate the number of **daisies** on his school field. He placed a 1 m^2 quadrat down at **eight random points** in the field and counted the number of daisies in each quadrat. He recorded his results in the table shown below.

Quadrat number	1	2	3	4	5	6	7	8
Number of daisies	3	1	2	1	4	3	0	2

a) What is a quadrat?

....

b) Suggest one way that Dan could make sure his quadrats are placed at random points.

....

....

c) **i)** Calculate the mean number of daisies per quadrat in the field.

....

ii) What is the median number of daisies per quadrat?

....

d) The total area of the field is 5 600 m^2.
Use your answer to **c) i)** to estimate the number of daisies in the whole of the field.

....

Top Tips: Some questions may feel like you're doing maths rather than biology... but you can't get away from things like averages — you do need to know how to work them out for the exam. Booo.

More on the Distribution of Organisms

Q1 Sandy uses a **transect** to investigate buttercup distribution from the middle of a field to a pond.

a) **i)** On the diagram below, draw **one** way that Sandy could set up her transect.

ii) Describe how Sandy could use the transect you've drawn above in her investigation.

....

....

b) Give **one** way in which Sandy could make her results more reliable.

....

c) The results of Sandy's investigation are shown in the table below.

Distance away from pond (m)	2	4	6	8	10
Number of buttercups per m^2	26	19	14	9	5

i) Describe the **correlation** between the number of buttercups and the distance from the pond.

....

ii) Suggest a reason for the correlation.

....

....

Q2 Bill carried out a similar investigation to Sandy's in a field next to a wood. Between the edge of the wood and the field is a small stream. Bill found the number of **dandelions** decreased from the middle of the field to the wood. He wanted to see if the difference in distribution of dandelions was due to a difference in **light intensity**, so he measured light intensity and found it also decreased towards the wood.

Explain why Bill's data isn't valid.

....

....

....

Mixed Questions — Biology 2a

Q1 Draw lines to match up the words below with their correct definition.

Tissue	The place where an organism lives.
Diffusion	The process that produces 'food' (glucose) in plants and algae.
Habitat	Something that stops photosynthesis from happening any faster.
Mode	A group of similar cells that work together to carry out a certain function.
Photosynthesis	The process by which cells become specialised for a particular job.
Limiting factor	The most common value in a set of data.
Differentiation	The spreading out of particles from an area of high concentration to an area of low concentration.

Q2 Cells in **plants** are different from cells in animals.

a) Name **three** parts that are found in plant cells but **not** in animal cells.

1. .... 2. .... 3. ....

b) Palisade cells are a type of plant cell.

i) Complete this diagram of a palisade cell by filling in the labels.

....

....

....

....

ii) State **one** visible feature of the **palisade cell** shown above and explain how it helps the cell to do its job.

Feature: ....

Function of this feature: ....

....

Mixed Questions — Biology 2a

Q3 Plants use photosynthesis to produce glucose.

a) Name the substance in a plant that absorbs light energy during photosynthesis.

....

b) Circle **two** raw materials needed for photosynthesis from the options given below.

carbon dioxide oxygen food water nitrogen helium

c) Plants store some of the glucose for use when photosynthesis isn't happening.

i) What do plants store glucose as? ....

ii) Name **one** place in a plant where the glucose is stored.

....

d) Other than storage, give **three uses** of glucose for plants.

1. ....

2. ....

3. ....

Q4 **Animals** are made up of cells, tissues, organs and organ systems.

a) Name the part(s) of a typical animal cell:

i) where energy is released from glucose, ...

ii) where most of the chemical reactions happen. ....

b) What does muscular tissue do?

....

c) Describe the **function** of the following organs:

i) the small intestine ....

ii) the large intestine ....

d) Label the following organs on the picture of part of the digestive system:

i) the pancreas

ii) the liver

Mixed Questions — Biology 2a

Q5 A student was given **three solutions** labelled X, Y and Z. He set up the experiment shown below and left it for a day. At the end of the experiment, the water outside the membrane contained particles X and Y, but not Z.

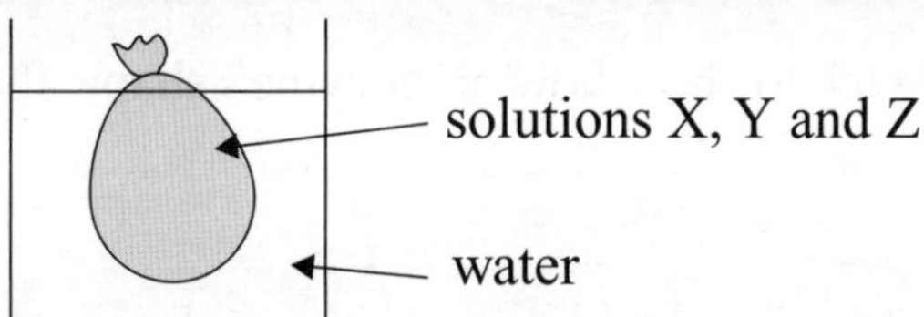

a) Name the process by which particles of X and Y moved through the membrane.

....

b) What can you conclude about the relative sizes of the X, Y and Z particles?

....

c) Solutions X, Y and Z were in fact amino acid, protein and glucose solutions. Which of these solutions was substance Z? Explain your answer.

....

....

Q6 Some students wanted to estimate the size of the population of **clover plants** around their school.

a) What piece of equipment should they use?

....

b) The school field is 250 m long by 180 m wide. Hannah counted 11 clover plants in a 1 m^2 area of the field. Approximately how many clover plants are there likely to be on the whole field?

....

c) Lisa decided to collect data from five different 1 m^2 areas of the school field. Her results are shown in the table below.

	Area 1	Area 2	Area 3	Area 4	Area 5
No. of plants	11	9	8	9	7

i) Calculate the **mean** number of clover plants per m^2 in Lisa's survey.

....

ii) Use Lisa's data to estimate the population size of clover plants on the field.

....

d) Whose estimation of population size is likely to be more accurate? Explain your answer.

....

Enzymes

Q1 a) Write a definition of the word '**enzyme**'.

....

b) In the space below draw a sketch to show how an enzyme's **shape** allows it to break substances down.

Q2 Complete the passage about **proteins** using some of the words given below.

increases catalyst high fats hormones
amino acids decreases proteins structural body sugars

A .... is a substance which .... the speed of a reaction without being changed or used up. Enzymes catalyse the useful reactions going on inside cells. All enzymes are .... , which are molecules made up of long chains of .... These chains fold up into the specific shapes that enzymes need to do their jobs. Proteins also act as .... components of tissues, ... and antibodies.

Q3 This graph shows the results from an investigation into the effect of **temperature** on the rate of an **enzyme** catalysed reaction.

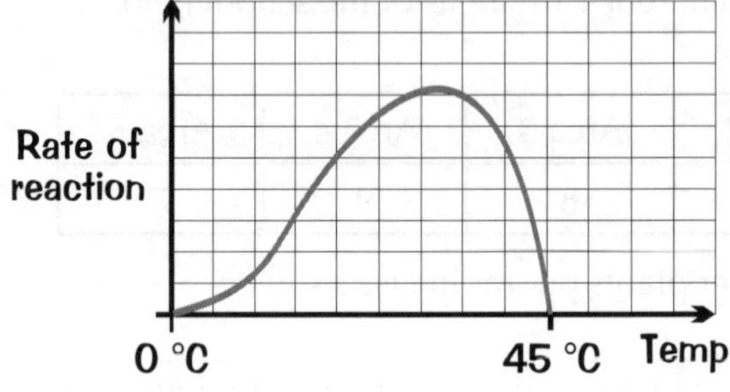

a) What is the **optimum** temperature for this enzyme?

....

b) What happens to enzymes at temperatures **above** their optimum?

....

Enzymes

Q4 Stuart has a sample of an enzyme and he is trying to find out what its **optimum pH** is. Stuart tests the enzyme by **timing** how long it takes to break down a substance at different pH levels. The results of Stuart's experiment are shown below.

pH	time taken for reaction in seconds
2	101
4	83
6	17
8	76
10	99
12	102

a) Draw a line graph of the results on the grid below.

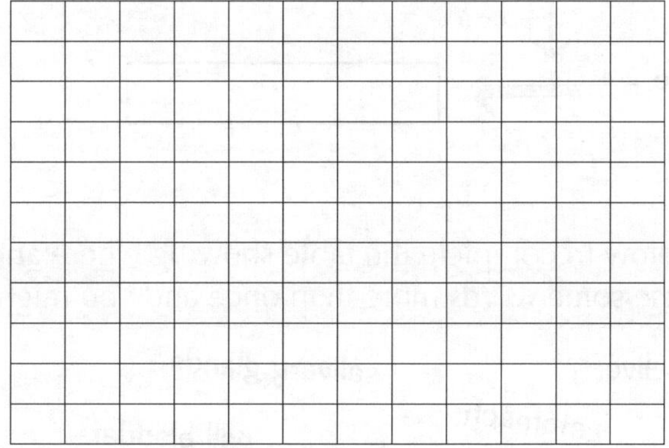

b) Roughly what is the **optimum** pH for the enzyme?

....

c) Explain why the reaction is very slow at certain pH levels.

....

....

d) Would you expect to find this enzyme in the stomach? Explain your answer.

....

e) Describe two things that Stuart would need to do to make sure his experiment is a fair test.

1. ....

2. ....

Top Tips: Enzymes crop up a lot in Biology so it's worth spending plenty of time making sure you know all the basics. If you're finding things a bit dull, you could always take a little break and eat some tofu to make sure you have enough protein to make lots of delightful enzymes.

Enzymes and Digestion

Q1 Fill in the boxes to show how the **three main food groups** are **broken down** during digestion.

a)

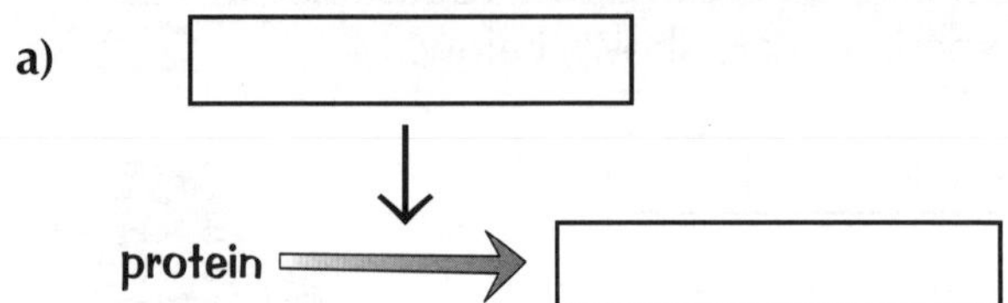

b)

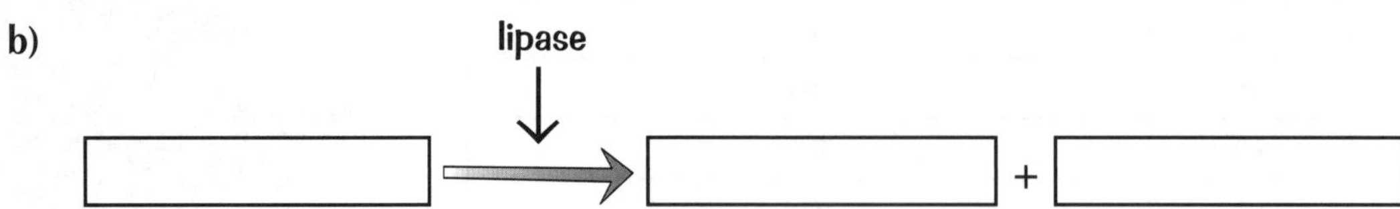

c)

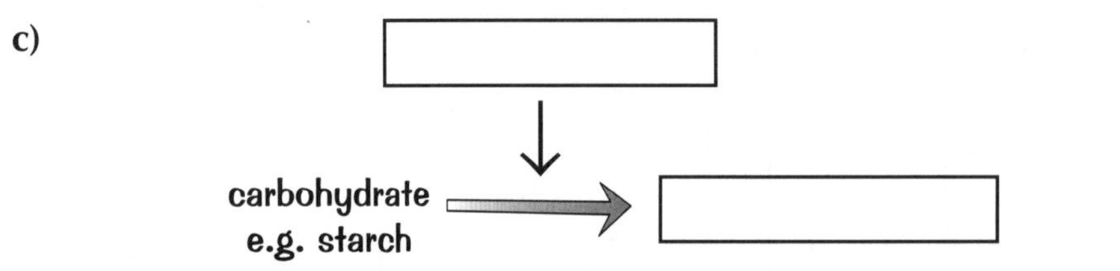

Q2 Choose from the words below to complete the table showing where **amylase**, **protease**, **lipase** and **bile** are made. You may use some words more than once and you might not need some of them.

pancreas liver salivary glands small intestine
large intestine stomach gall bladder kidneys

Amylase	Protease	Lipase	Bile

Q3 a) Circle the correct words from each pair to complete this passage about **bile**.

Bile is stored in the **gall bladder** / **pancreas** before being released into the **liver** / **small intestine**. Bile **acidifies** / **neutralises** the material from the stomach which provides the optimum pH for the **enzymes** / **microorganisms** in the rest of the digestive system to work. Bile breaks **fat** / **glycerol** into smaller droplets.

b) Explain how emulsification helps digestion.

....

....

More on Enzymes and Digestion

Q1 Fill in the boxes to label this diagram of the human **digestive system**.

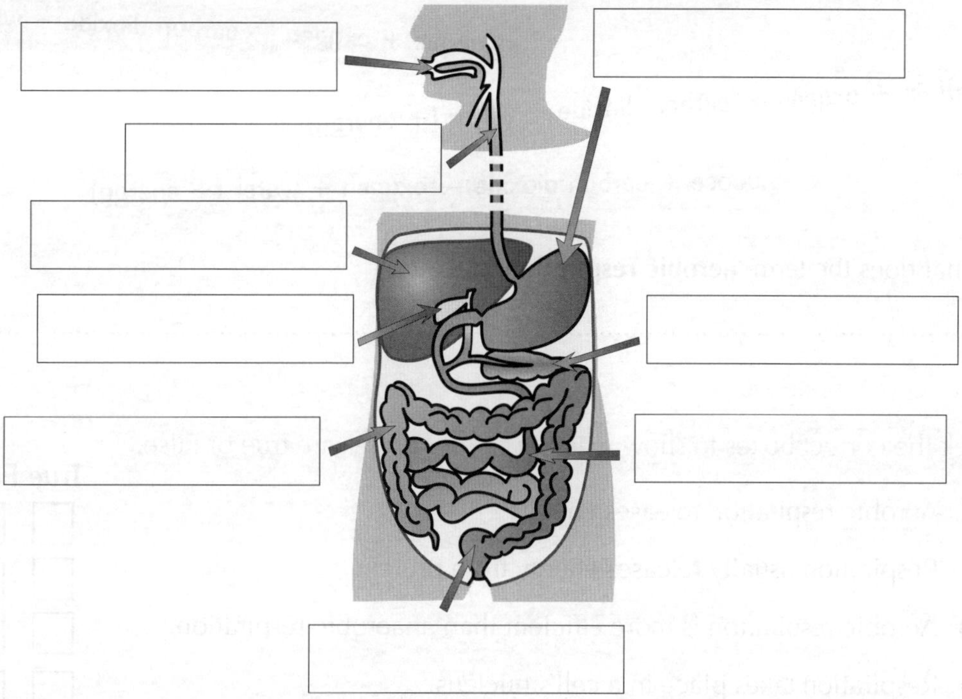

Q2 Tick the correct boxes to show whether the following sentences about **digestion** are **true** or **false**.

		True	False
a)	**Hydrochloric acid** is produced by the liver.	☐	☐
b)	Some digestive enzymes are made by special cells in **glands** and then released into the gut.	☐	☐
c)	Specialised cells in the **lining of the gut** can also produce digestive enzymes.	☐	☐
d)	**Pepsin** works best in alkaline conditions.	☐	☐

Q3 Describe the role of each of the following in **digestion**:

a) Salivary glands

....

b) Pancreas

....

c) Liver

....

Top Tips: This stuff is pretty easy so it shouldn't take you long to learn. The trickiest bits are probably the roles of the liver and pancreas — make sure you've got those clear in your head.

Enzymes and Respiration

Q1 a) Circle the correct word equation for **aerobic respiration**.

glucose + oxygen → carbon dioxide + water (+ energy)

protein + oxygen → carbon dioxide + water (+ energy)

glucose + carbon dioxide → oxygen + water (+ energy)

b) What does the term '**aerobic respiration**' mean?

....

Q2 a) Tick the correct boxes to show whether the sentences are true or false.

	True	False
i) Aerobic respiration releases energy.	☐	☐
ii) Respiration usually releases energy from protein.	☐	☐
iii) Aerobic respiration is more efficient than anaerobic respiration.	☐	☐
iv) Respiration takes place in a cell's nucleus.	☐	☐
v) Aerobic respiration produces carbon dioxide.	☐	☐
vi) Breathing is a kind of respiration.	☐	☐
vii) Respiration goes on all the time in both plants and animals.	☐	☐
viii) Respiration involves reactions catalysed by enzymes.	☐	☐

b) Write a correct version of each false sentence in the space below.

....

....

....

Q3 Give **four** examples of things that animals and / or plants use **energy** for.

1. ....
2. ....
3. ....
4. ....

Top Tips: Hmm, respiration, there isn't really much to say other than make sure you learn the word equation and remember that IT'S NOT THE SAME AS BREATHING.

Exercise

Q1 Complete the following sentences by circling the correct words from each pair.

a) During exercise our muscles need more **energy** / **water** to enable them to keep **relaxing** / **contracting**.

b) This means they need a continuous supply of **protein** / **glucose** and **carbon dioxide** / **oxygen**.

c) During vigorous exercise muscles use glucose **slowly** / **rapidly**, so some of the stored **glycogen** / **oxygen** is converted back to glucose to provide more energy.

d) If your body can't supply enough oxygen to the muscles during exercise they start doing **aerobic** / **anaerobic** respiration.

e) Anaerobic respiration is the **complete** / **incomplete** breakdown of glucose.

Q2 John has to **sprint** for the bus because he is late.

a) State **two** effects this sudden physical exercise has on John's body.

1. ....

2. ....

b) After his initial sprint, John's leg muscles become tired and stop contracting efficiently.

i) What name is given to this effect? ....

ii) Suggest the substance that is causing this effect. ....

iii) What **process** produces this substance? ....

c) When he gets on the bus he's out of breath.
Explain why he continues to breathe deeply for a while.

....

....

....

Q3 a) Use some of the words given below to complete the word equation for **anaerobic respiration**.

carbon dioxide **oxygen** **lactic acid** **water** **glucose** **energy**

Anaerobic: .... → .... (+ ....)

b) Does anaerobic respiration produce **more** or **less** energy than aerobic respiration?

....

Exercise

Q4 Jim is a keen runner. He takes part in a 400 metre race. The **graph** below shows Jim's **breathing rate** before, during and after the race.

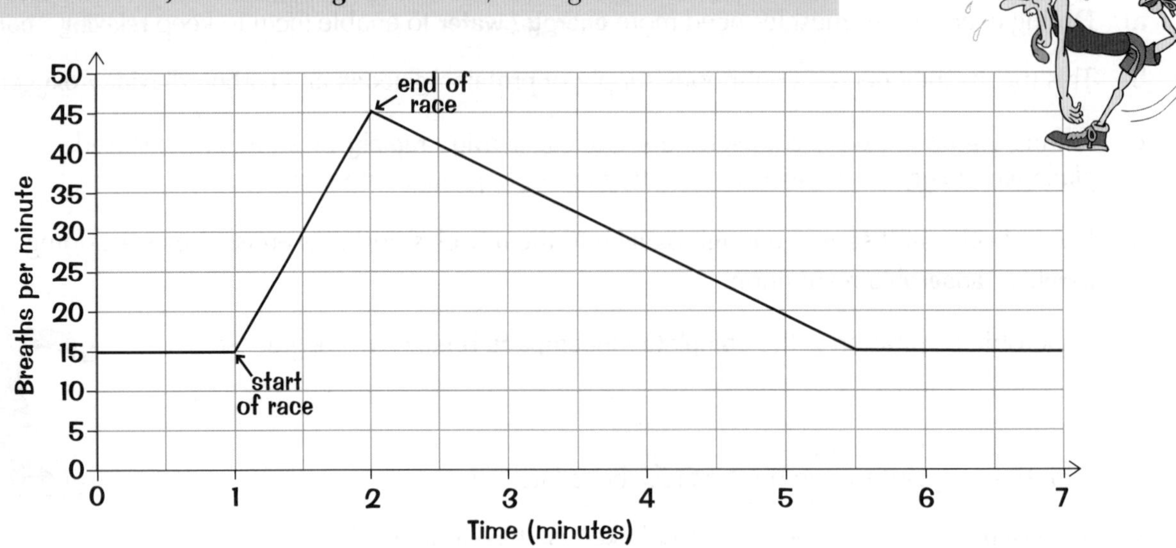

a) How much does Jim's breathing rate go up during the race? .... **breaths per minute**

b) Explain why exercise makes Jim's breathing rate increase.

....

....

....

c) How long does it take for Jim's breathing rate return to normal after the race?

....

Q5 Roy wants to find out which of his friends has the shortest **'recovery' time**. Your recovery time is how long it takes for your pulse rate to **return to normal** after exercise. Roy tests his friends separately. He measures their **pulse rate**, then asks them to **run** for 2 minutes. After they've finished running, he measures their pulse rate at 15 second intervals until it has returned to normal.

a) Write down **two** things Roy should do to ensure it is a **fair test**.

Think about keeping things constant.

1. ....

....

2. ....

b) Here is a sketch of Roy's results. Which of his friends had the **shortest** recovery time?

....

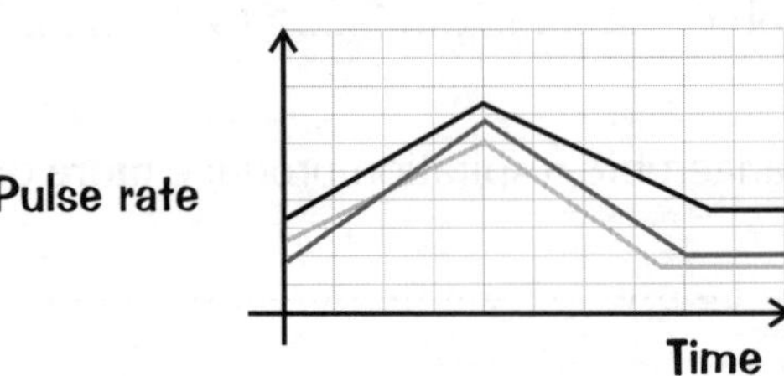

Uses of Enzymes

Q1 **Enzymes** are often used in industrial processes to alter foods. Explain how enzymes can be used in making:

a) baby foods.

....

....

b) 'slimming' foods.

....

....

....

Q2 The picture below shows two types of **washing powder**.

Lipaclean
Contains lipase enzymes

Protewash
packed with proteases

a) Which of the two washing powders would you recommend to someone who has dripped **butter** on their shirt? Explain your answer.

....

....

b) Why are some people unable to use washing powders like these?

....

Q3 Complete the following sentences by circling the correct words from each pair.

a) Starch and sugar are both **proteins / carbohydrates / fats**.

b) Starch syrup **is / isn't** sweet. Sugar syrup **is / isn't** sweet.

c) You can convert starch syrup into sugar syrup by adding **lipases / carbohydrases / proteases**.

Uses of Enzymes

Q4 **Enzymes** are often used in **industrial processes**.

a) Why are enzymes used in industrial processes?

....

b) Name **two** conditions that need to be carefully controlled for the enzymes to work efficiently.

1. ....

2. ....

c) **i)** Give **two advantages** of using enzymes in industry.

1. ....

....

2. ....

....

ii) Give **one disadvantage** of using enzymes in industry.

....

....

Q5 Caroline is testing the effectiveness of two different **washing powders** at getting out food stains. She washes stained clothes in both powders, at different temperatures. Then she records their **effectiveness** using a scale of **1** (**poor**) to **10** (**excellent**).

a) Name **one** thing that Caroline must do to make sure that her experiment is a fair test.

....

b) Caroline's results are shown in the table on the right.

i) State which powder is best at cleaning food stains at 30 °C.

....

ii) Which of the powders is a **biological detergent**? Explain your answer.

....

....

		Washing powder	
		A	**B**
Effectiveness	**Temperature: 20 °C**	5	2
	Temperature: 30 °C	8	4
	Temperature: 40 °C	9	6

Top Tips: Each enzyme catalyses a specific reaction, e.g. proteases break down proteins. This means enzymes can be really useful, e.g. proteases are put in biological detergents. However, when using them, you have to keep conditions tightly controlled otherwise they will be denatured.

DNA

Q1 DNA contains all the **instructions** to make an living organism.

a) What does DNA stand for? ....deoxyribonucleic acid....

b) Fill in the blanks in the paragraph below using words from the list.

cells chromosomes cytoplasm gene amino acids section protein fat

DNA is found in the nucleus of animal and plant .... in very long molecules called .... A gene is a .... of DNA. Each gene contains instructions for the cell to make a specific .... Cells make proteins by connecting .... together in a particular order.

c) How many amino acids are used to make proteins in the human body? ....20........

d) DNA molecules have a special twisted structure. Give the name of this structure.

....

e) Is everyone's DNA unique? Explain your answer.

....

Q2 **Genetic fingerprinting** is a way of comparing people's DNA — it's useful in forensic science. Put these following stages of DNA fingerprinting into the correct order.

Compare the unique patterns of DNA.

Collect the sample for DNA testing.

Separate the sections of DNA.

Cut the DNA into small sections.

1. ....
2. ....
3. ....
4. ....

Q3 A national **genetic database** would allow everyone's unique pattern of DNA to be saved on file.

a) Give one use of a national genetic database.

....

b) Give one drawback of a national genetic database.

....

DNA

Q4 A thoroughbred horse breeder has collected DNA samples from each of her horses. Her **new foal's DNA** is **sample 1**. The **mother** of the foal provided **sample 2**. Study the **DNA profiles** and complete the table showing which horse is the **foal's father**.

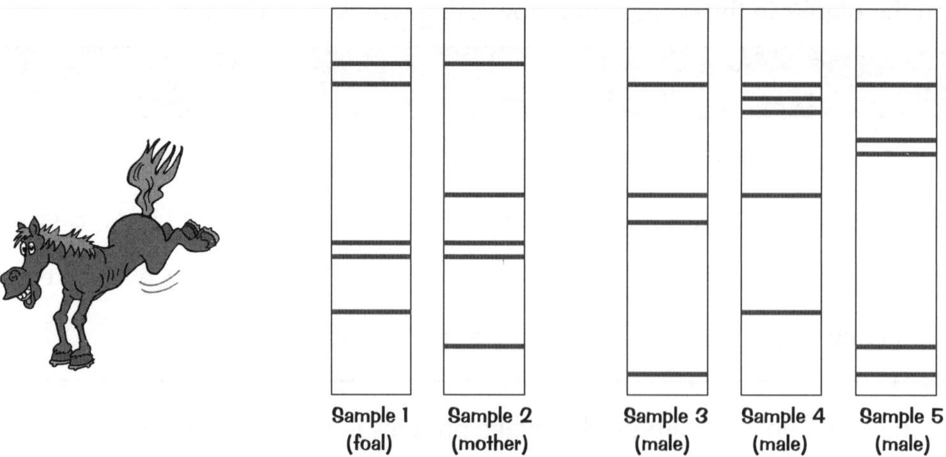

	Foal	Mother	Father
DNA sample	Sample 1	Sample 2	

Q5 The following **DNA samples** are being used in a **murder investigation**. The DNA samples are from the victim, three suspects and some blood which was found on the victim's shirt.

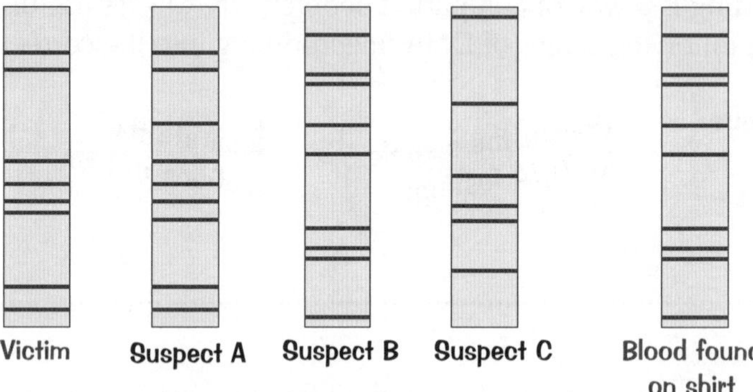

a) Which two individuals are likely to be **related** to each other? Explain your choice.

....

b) Who is the most likely suspect based on the DNA evidence? ....

c) How do you know?

....

d) Can this suspect be accused of murder beyond all doubt? Explain your answer.

....

....

Cell Division — Mitosis

Q1 Decide whether the following statements are **true** or **false**.

		True	False
a)	There are 46 chromosomes in most of your body cells.		
b)	There are 20 pairs of chromosomes in a human cheek cell.		
c)	Chromosomes are found in the cytoplasm of a cell.		
d)	Before a cell divides by mitosis, it duplicates its DNA.		
e)	Mitosis is where a cell splits to create two genetically identical copies.		
f)	Mitosis produces new cells to replace those which are damaged.		
g)	We need mitosis to grow.		

Q2 The following diagrams show the different stages of **mitosis**.
Draw lines to match the description of each stage with the correct diagram.

a)

b)

c)

d)

e)

A membrane forms in each half of the cell to form the nuclei.

Cells that are not dividing contain long strings of DNA.

The cytoplasm divides, making two new genetically identical cells.

The chromosomes line up across the centre of the cell, and then the arms of each chromosome are pulled to opposite ends of the cell.

Before a cell divides, it copies (duplicates) its DNA and forms X-shaped chromosomes.

Q3 Complete the following passage using the words below.

runners **strawberry** **variation** **asexual** **reproduce** **genes**

Some organisms use mitosis to .... For example, ... plants produce .... this way, which become new plants.

This is known as .... reproduction. The offspring have exactly the same .... as the parent, which means there's no genetic ....

Cell Division — Meiosis

Q1 Tick the boxes below to show which statements are true of **meiosis**.

		True	False
a)	Halves the number of chromosomes.	☐	☐
b)	Chromosomes line up in the centre of the cell.	☐	☐
c)	Forms cells that are genetically different.	☐	☐
d)	In humans, it only happens in the reproductive organs.	☐	☐
e)	Doesn't form gametes.	☐	☐

Q2 Draw lines to match the descriptions of the stages of **meiosis** to the right diagrams below.

a)

b)

c)

d)

e)

The pairs are pulled apart. Each new cell has only one copy of each chromosome, some from the mother and some from the father.

Before the cell starts to divide it duplicates its DNA to produce an exact copy.

There are now 4 gametes, each containing half the original number of chromosomes.

For the first meiotic division the chromosomes line up in their pairs across the centre of the cell.

The chromosomes line up across the centre of the nucleus ready for the second division, and the left and right arms are pulled apart.

Q3 Circle the correct words from each pair to complete these sentences about **sexual reproduction**.

a) Sexual reproduction involves genetic material from **one** / **two** individual(s).

b) In humans, body cells contain **46** / **23** chromosomes and sex cells contain **46** / **23** chromosomes.

c) Sexual reproduction produces offspring with **identical** / **different** genes to the parent.

d) The sperm cell contains **the same number of** / **half as many** chromosomes as the **fertilised** egg.

Top Tips: It's easy to get confused between mitosis and meiosis. Mitosis occurs in asexual reproduction and makes clones. Meiosis is for sexual reproduction and creates sex cells.

Cell Division — Meiosis

Q4 Mosquitoes have **three pairs** of **chromosomes** in their body cells.
The diagram below shows a mosquito cell that is about to divide by **meiosis**.

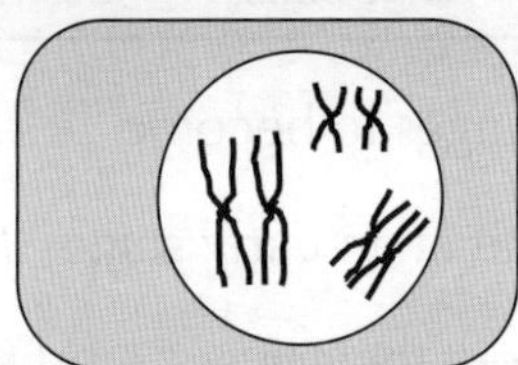

Below, draw the chromosomes in one of the cells produced from this cell:

a) after the first division stage of meiosis.

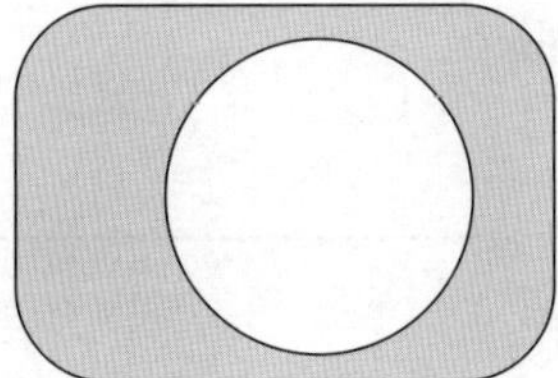

b) after the second division stage of meiosis.

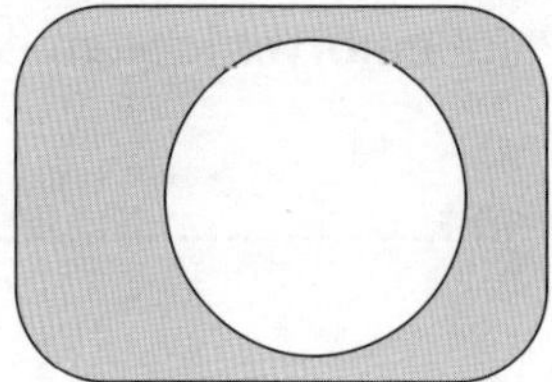

Q5 At fertilisation, two **gametes** combine to form a new individual.

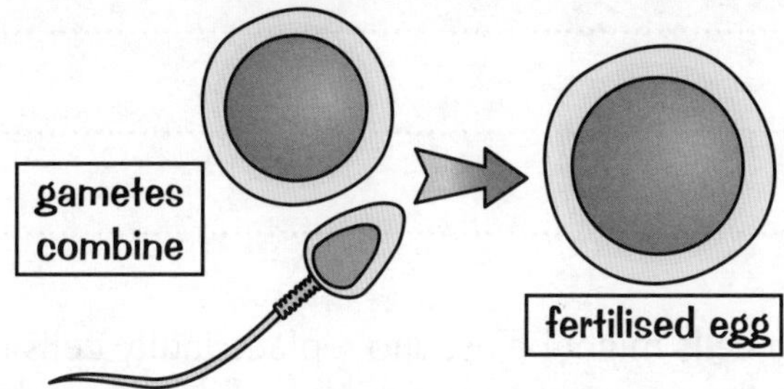

a) What are gametes?

....

b) Explain why gametes have half the usual number of chromosomes.

....

....

c) Explain how sexual reproduction gives rise to **variation**.

....

....

....

d) After fertilisation, by what process does the fertilised egg divide?

....

Stem Cells

Q1 Complete the following passage about **differentiation** using words from the list below.

plant **embryos** **specialised** **sex cells** **stem cells** **animal**

Differentiation is the way in which a cell changes to become .... for its job. .... cells usually differentiate at an early stage. Most .... cells keep the ability to differentiate throughout their lives. Undifferentiated cells that can develop into many different types of cell are called ....

Q2 How are **embryonic** stem cells different from **adult** stem cells?

....

....

Q3 Describe a way that stem cells are already used in medicine.

....

....

....

Q4 In the future, **embryonic stem cells** might be used to replace faulty cells in sick people. Match the problems below to the potential cures which could be made with stem cells.

diabetes	**heart muscle cells**
paralysis	**insulin-producing cells**
heart disease	**nerve cells**

Q5 People have **different opinions** when it comes to **stem cell research**.

a) Give one argument **in favour** of stem cell research.

....

....

b) Give one argument **against** stem cell research.

....

....

X and Y Chromosomes

Q1 Tick the boxes to show whether each statement is **true** or **false**.

		True	False
a)	Women have two X chromosomes. Men have an X and a Y chromosome.		
b)	There is a 75% chance that a couple's first child will be a girl.		
c)	Sperm cells (male gametes) can carry an X or a Y chromosome.		
d)	If you have 4 children, you will always get 2 boys and 2 girls.		

Q2 Here is a genetic diagram showing the inheritance of **sex chromosomes** in humans.

a) Complete the diagram to show the combinations of chromosomes in the offspring.

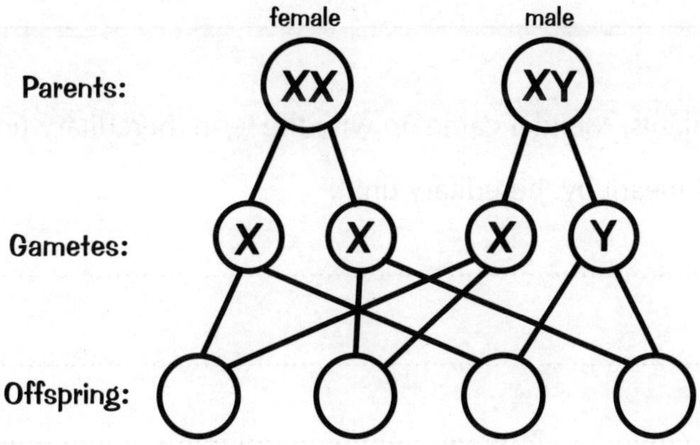

female male

Parents: XX XY

Gametes: X X X Y

Offspring:

b) A woman becomes pregnant. What is the probability that the embryo is **male**?

....

Q3 **Birds** have sex chromosomes called **Z** and **W** (just like humans have X and Y). In birds, those with **two Z chromosomes** are **male**.

a) What are the female bird's sex chromosomes?

....

b) Complete the genetic diagram below to show the possible combination of gametes in bird reproduction.

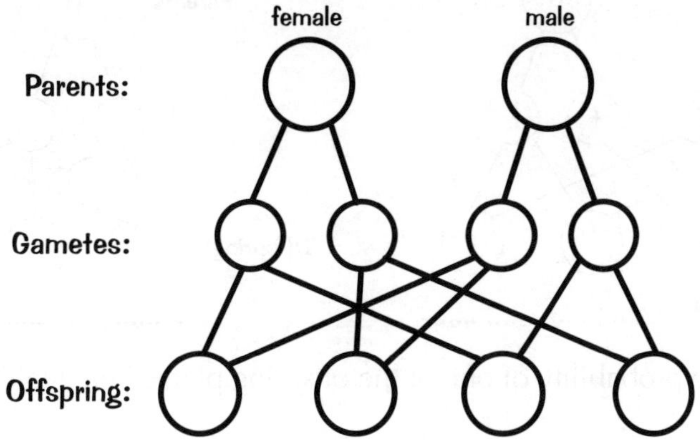

female male

Parents:

Gametes:

Offspring:

The Work of Mendel

Q1 Use words from the following list to complete the paragraph below.

leaf **genetics** **monk** **double-glazing salesman** **1866** **viruses**

physicist **characteristics** **1980** **generation** **bulbs**

Gregor Mendel was a .... Mendel observed plants in his garden. He realised that .... in plants are passed on from one .... to the next. He published his findings in .... Mendel is regarded by many people as the father of modern ....

Q2 After observing pea plants, Mendel came up with the term 'hereditary unit'.

a) Explain what Mendel meant by 'hereditary unit'.

....

....

....

b) Mendel said that some hereditary units were **dominant** and some were **recessive**.
If an organism has both the dominant and the recessive hereditary units for a characteristic, which is expressed?

....

Q3 Mendel crossed different combinations of **tall** and **dwarf** pea plants.

a) Complete the genetic diagrams below showing crossings of different pea plants.
T represents the dominant allele for **tall plants** and **t** represents the recessive allele for **dwarf plants**.

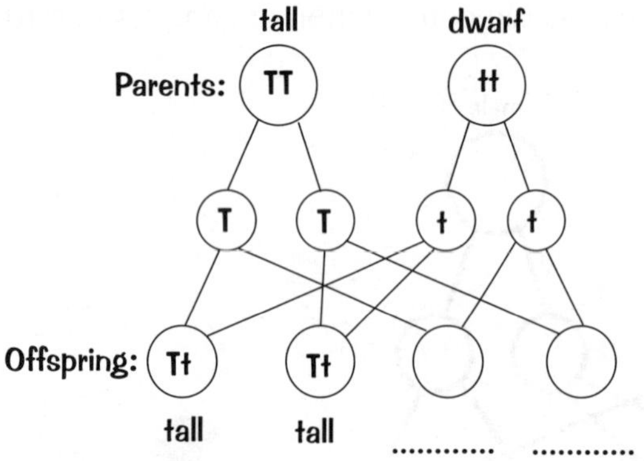

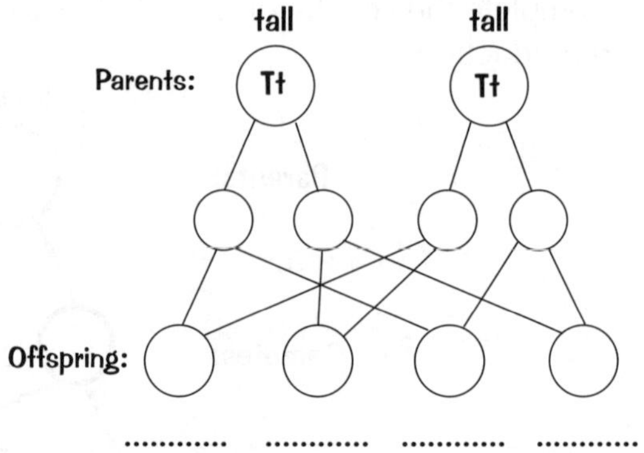

b) In **cross 2**, what is the probability of one of the offspring plants being tall?

....

Genetic Diagrams

Q1 Draw lines to match each of the terms below with its meaning.

dominant	having two different alleles for a gene
genotype	having two identical alleles for a gene
heterozygous	shown in organisms heterozygous for that trait
homozygous	not shown in organisms heterozygous for that trait
phenotype	the actual characteristics of an individual
recessive	the alleles that an individual contains

Q2 Wilma carries a **recessive** allele for **red** hair and a **dominant** allele for **brown** hair.

a) What is Wilma's natural hair colour?

....

b) Is Wilma homozygous or heterozygous for this characteristic?

....

Q3 Fruit flies usually have **red** eyes. However, there are a small number of white-eyed fruit flies. Having **white** eyes is a **recessive** characteristic.

a) Complete the following sentences with either '**red eyes**' or '**white eyes**'.

i) **R** is the allele for ....

ii) **r** is the allele for ....

iii) Fruit flies with alleles **RR** or **Rr** will have ....

iv) Fruit flies with the alleles **rr** will have ....

b) Two fruit flies have the alleles **Rr**. They fall in love and get it on.

i) Complete this genetic diagram to show the possible offspring. One's been done for you.

parent's alleles	**R**	**r**
R	RR	
r		

(rows: parent's alleles; columns: parent's alleles)

Read down and across to work out what combination of alleles should be in each box.

ii) What is the probability that the fruit flies' offspring will have **white eyes**?

....

iii) The fruit flies have 16 offspring. How many of the offspring are **likely** to have **red eyes**?

....

Genetic Diagrams

Q4 Seeds of pea plants can be **smooth** or **wrinkled**. The allele for smooth seeds (**S**) is dominant. The allele for wrinkled seeds (**s**) is recessive.

a) The diagrams below shows a cross between a thoroughbred pea plant with smooth seeds (genetic type **SS**) and a thoroughbred pea plant with wrinkled seeds (genetic type **ss**).

Complete the genetic diagram.

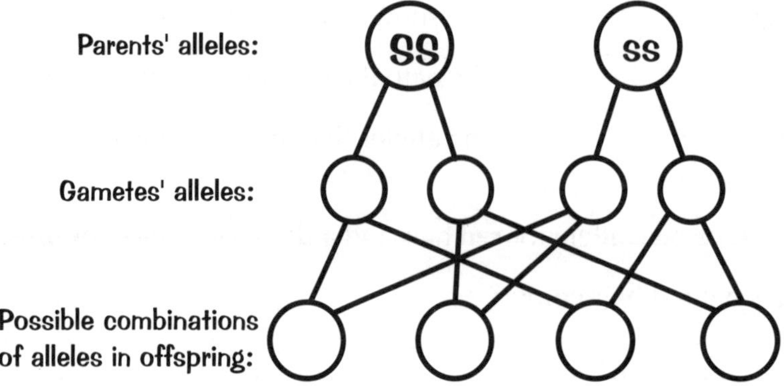

b) In this cross, what is the probability of one offspring producing wrinkled seeds? Tick the correct option.

- ☐ 100% chance of producing wrinkled seeds
- ☐ 50% chance of producing wrinkled seeds
- ☐ 25% chance of producing wrinkled seeds
- ☐ 0% chance of producing wrinkled seeds

Pictures of peas are very dull.
So here's a picture of a tapir instead.

c) Two hybrid pea plants (**Ss**) are interbred.
Complete the genetic diagram to show the possible combinations of alleles in the offspring.

	parent's alleles: S	parent's alleles: s
parent's alleles: S		
parent's alleles: s		

d) Is the following statement **true** or **false**? Tick the correct box.

"Mrs Maguire crosses two pea plants with the alleles Ss. If she gets 12 new seedlings as a result, it's most likely that 3 of the seedlings will produce wrinkled seeds."

True ☐ False ☐

Top Tips: Genetic diagrams look like alphabet spaghetti at first — but they're OK really. They're useful for working out the possible combinations of alleles that offspring can get from their parents — and the probability of each combination.

Genetic Disorders

Q1 **Cystic fibrosis** is a **genetic disorder** which affects cell membranes.
It is caused by a **recessive** allele, which can be passed on from parents to their children.

a) Complete the following genetic diagram showing the inheritance of cystic fibrosis.
The recessive allele for cystic fibrosis is **f**, and the dominant allele is **F**.

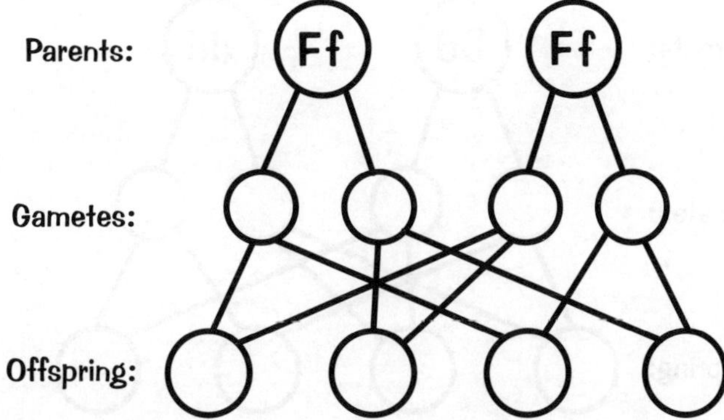

b) **i)** In the above genetic diagram, what is the probability of a child having cystic fibrosis?

....

ii) In the above genetic diagram, what is the probability of a child being a carrier of the cystic fibrosis allele (but not having the disease)?

....

c) Approximately **1 in every 2500** babies born in the UK will have cystic fibrosis. About 600 000 babies are born in the UK each year. How many would you expect to have cystic fibrosis?

....

Q2 John is a carrier of **cystic fibrosis**, a **recessive** genetic disorder. His wife Helen is **not** a carrier of cystic fibrosis (and does not suffer from the disease).

a) John and Helen are planning a family.

i) Complete the genetic diagram on the right to show what alleles their child might inherit from them.

Use the symbols **F** and **f** to represent the alleles.

Helen's alleles

John's alleles

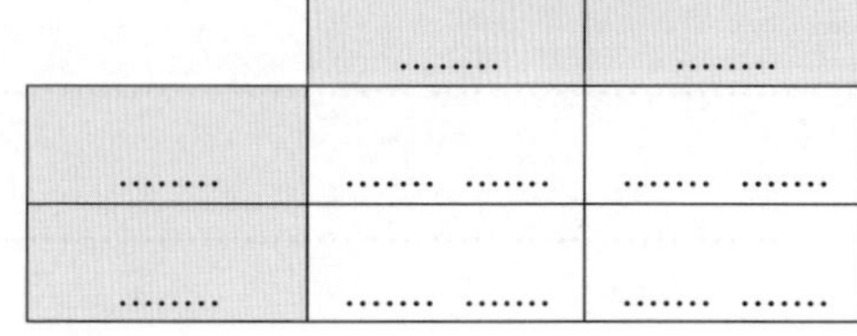

ii) What is the probability that John and Helen's child will suffer from cystic fibrosis?

....

b) John's brother Mark suffers from cystic fibrosis. Mark's wife is **not** a carrier or a sufferer.
Could a child of theirs suffer from cystic fibrosis? Explain your answer.

....

....

Genetic Disorders

Q3 **Polydactyly** is a **genetic disorder** which causes a baby to be born with **extra fingers or toes**. Polydactyly is caused by a **dominant** allele.

a) **i)** Complete the genetic diagram below showing the inheritance pattern of polydactyly. The dominant allele for polydactyly is **D**, and the recessive allele is **d**.

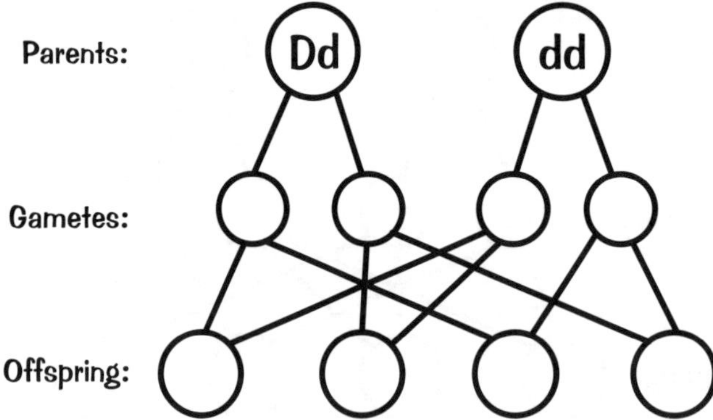

ii) In the above genetic diagram, what is the probability that a child will be polydactyl?

....

b) Will a person with the alleles **Dd** be a **sufferer**, a **carrier** or **neither**? Explain your answer.

....

....

c) State the probability that of a child of two parents with the alleles **DD** and **dd** will be polydactyl.

....

Q4 During in vitro fertilisation (IVF) a cell can be removed from an embryo and **screened** for **genetic disorders**. If a faulty allele is present, the embryo is destroyed.

a) Explain why some people think embryo screening is a **bad** thing.

....

....

....

b) Explain why some people think embryo screening is a **good** thing.

....

....

....

More Genetic Diagrams

Q1 An allele for the colour grey (**G**) in mice is dominant over the allele for the colour white (**g**). A hybrid grey mouse (**Gg**) was bred with a thoroughbred white mouse (**gg**).

a) Complete the genetic diagram below to show the potential combinations of alleles in the offspring of the two mice.

Parents: Gg gg

Gametes:

Offspring:

'Hybrid' = an organism which has two different alleles for the same characteristic, e.g. Hh.
Thoroughbred = an organism which has two identical alleles for a characteristic, e.g. HH or hh.

b) What is the likely ratio of colours in any litters of offspring (grey : white)?

....

c) If the mice had 12 babies, how many would there be **likely** to be of each colour?

....

Q2 Sally is investigating the inheritance of **flower colours**. She knows that the allele for the colour **red** is **dominant** over the allele for the colour **white**.

Sally has two of the same plant, one with **red** flowers and one with **white** flowers. Suggest how Sally can find out whether the plant with red flowers is thoroughbred red (**RR**) or hybrid red (**Rr**).

....

....

....

....

Q3 An allele for the long hair (**H**) in cats is dominant over the allele for the short hair (**h**). A homozygous long-haired cat (**HH**) was bred with a homozygous short-haired cat (**hh**).

a) In the space below, draw a genetic diagram to show the potential combinations of alleles in the offspring of the two cats.

b) What is the probability of their offspring having:

i) long hair? ....

ii) short hair? ....

More Genetic Diagrams

Q4 The family tree below shows a family with a history of **cystic fibrosis**. Both Libby and Anne are pregnant. They know the sexes of their babies but not whether they have the disorder.

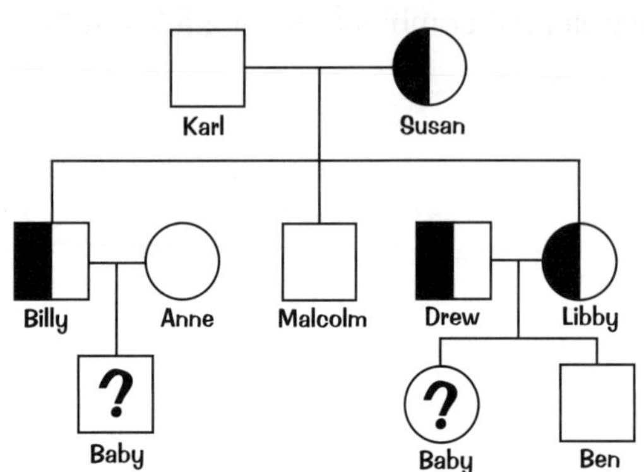

Key
Male
Female
Carrier
Sufferer

a) Explain how you can tell from the family tree that the allele for cystic fibrosis is **not** dominant.

....

....

....

....

b) Complete the table to show the percentage chances of Libby's and Anne's babies being carriers and sufferers.

Sketch a genetic diagram if it helps.

	Carrier	Sufferer
Libby		
Anne		

Q5 The family tree below shows a family with a history of **polydactyly**. Polydactyly is a dominant disorder. Individuals with the alleles **DD** or **Dd** will be **polydactyl**.

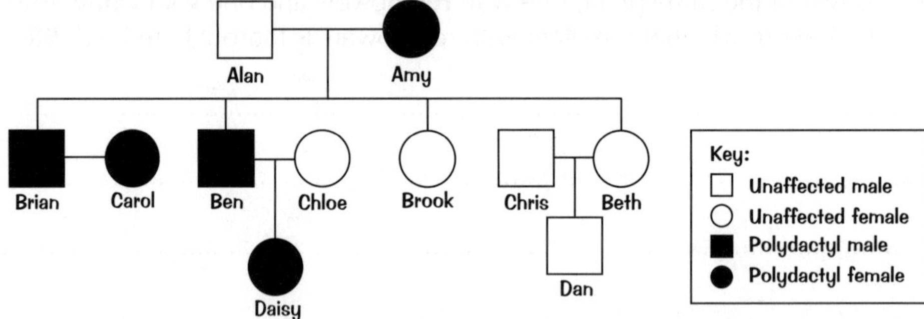

a) In the family tree, does **Amy** have the alleles **DD** or **Dd**? Explain your answer.

....

....

....

b) i) What alleles must **Brian** have? ....

Carol has the alleles **Dd**.

ii) Complete the genetic diagram on the right.

iii) Use your diagram to find the probability that a child of Brian and Carol's will **not** be polydactyl.

Probability: ....

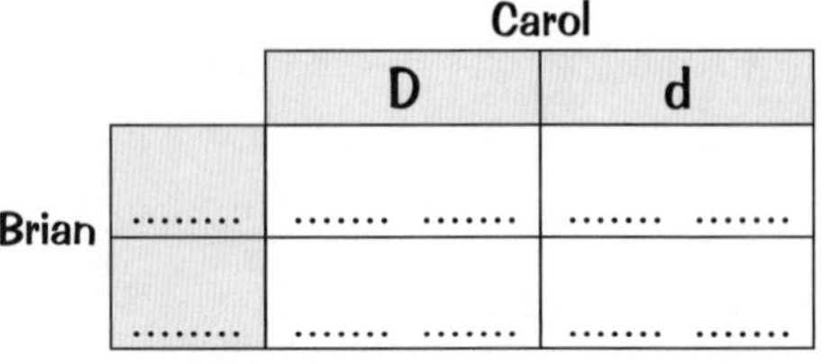

Fossils

Q1 Scientists can use **fossils** to study what life on Earth used to be like.

a) What is a fossil?

....

b) Where are fossils usually found?

....

Q2 Fossils are **formed** in several different ways.

Choose from the words provided to complete the passage about fossil formation.

cast	decays	bones	softens	tissues	shaped
clay	fast	hardens	sediments	slowly	rock

In one type of fossil formation, structures like teeth and .... decay very .... and are replaced by minerals that form a ....-like substance .... like the original structure.

In another type of fossil formation, a dead plant or animal is buried in a ....-like material which later ....

As the organism decays, a .... is left behind, leaving a clear impression.

Q3 **Fossils** can be formed in places where there is no decay such as in amber or tar pits.

a) **i)** What is amber?

....

ii) How exactly does amber preserve things?

....

b) Draw lines to match the reasons for no decay to the types of environment.

No oxygen or moisture	Peat bogs
Too acidic	Glaciers
Too cold	Tar pits

Pete's Bog

Fossils

Q4 It can be hard to find **fossils** of very **early life forms**.

Give **two** reasons why.

1. ....

....

2. ....

....

Q5 Fossils of shells were found in a sample of rock.

a) Explain how a shell lying in sediment at the bottom of the sea could be turned into a fossil.

....

....

....

Think about what replaces the tissues of organisms as they slowly decay.

b) Fossils were found in this sample of rock.
Explain why scientists think fossil B is older than fossil A.

Fossil A

Fossil B

....

....

....

Q6 One idea of **how life began** is that simple organic molecules were brought to Earth by **comets**. It's not known if this is right.

a) What do we call this type of scientific idea? ....

b) Suggest why this idea has neither been generally accepted or completely rejected by all scientists.

....

....

c) Give another scientific idea for how life began.

....

....

Top Tips: It's weird to think that looking at squiggles inside rocks (like the one above) can tell you what life used to be like ages ago... Don't forget to learn what fossils are and how they form.

Extinction and Speciation

Q1 Dinosaurs, mammoths and dodos are all animals that are now **extinct**.

a) What does the term 'extinct' mean?

....

....

b) How do we know about extinct animals?

....

....

Q2 There are many reasons why a species might become **extinct**.

Draw lines to match the reasons for extinction on the left with their correct examples on the right.

A catastrophic event kills every member of the species.

The environment changes too quickly.

A new disease kills every member of the species.

Every member of a species of toad is killed when a new fungal pathogen is accidentally introduced to their habitat.

Every member of a species of parrot becomes ill with a flu-like virus but then recovers.

An island's rainforest is completely chopped down, destroying the habitat of the striped monkey.

A rare plant that lives on the side of a volcano is wiped out when the volcano erupts.

Q3 A species is a group of similar organisms that can reproduce to give fertile offspring.

a) Define the term **speciation**.

....

b) How can you tell that speciation has occurred?

....

....

c) "Speciation can lead to extinction."
Tick the correct box to show whether this statement is **true** or **false**.

True ☐ False ☐

Extinction and Speciation

Q4 The diagrams below show the stages of **speciation**.
Draw lines to match the labels to the correct diagrams.

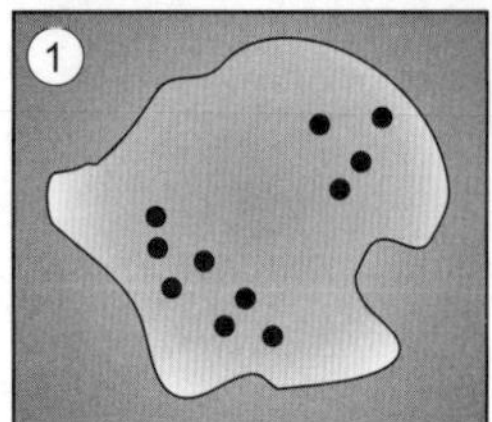

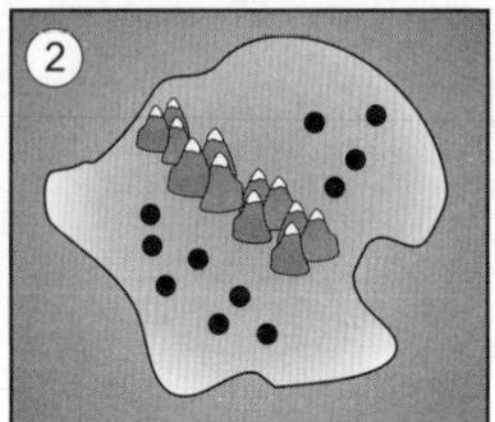

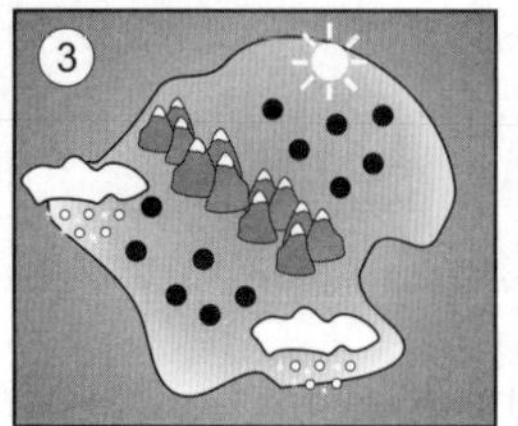

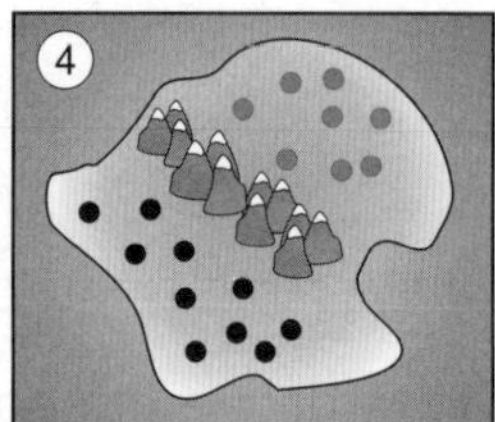

A new species develops.	The populations adapt to new environments.	There are two populations of the same species.	Physical barriers separate the populations.

Q5 **Purple banana-eating squirrels** used to found on one specific island but a scientist thinks that they've now become **extinct**. She looks into why this might have happened.

Briefly explain why each of these factors may have led to the squirrel population being wiped out.

a) A new population of **banana-eating spiders** was introduced to the island.

....

....

b) Ten **squirrel-eating gibbons** have escaped from the island zoo in the last five years.

....

....

Q6 **Isolation** and **natural selection** can lead to speciation.

a) What is meant by the term '**isolation**'?

....

b) The statements below describe how geographical isolation can lead to speciation.
Put them in the **correct order** by numbering the boxes. The first one has been done for you.

- [ ] The alleles that control the beneficial characteristics are more likely to be passed on to the next generation.
- [ ] Each population shows variation because they have a wide range of alleles.
- [ ] Eventually, individuals from the different populations have changed so much that they become separate species.
- [1] A physical barrier geographically isolates some individuals from the main population.
- [ ] In each population, individuals with characteristics that make them better adapted to their environment have a better chance of survival and so are more likely to breed successfully.
- [ ] Conditions on either side of a physical barrier are slightly different.

Mixed Questions — Biology 2b

Q1 **Stem cells** and their uses are a major focus of current medical research.

a) What unique characteristic do stem cells have which ordinary body cells don't have?

....

b) Scientists have experimented with growing stem cells in different conditions.

i) What is the name of the process by which stem cells **divide** for growth?

....

ii) Suggest why scientists are interested in **embryonic** stem cells.

....

....

c) Although there is potential for medical breakthroughs, some people disagree with stem cell research on ethical grounds. Describe one **ethical issue** surrounding stem cell research.

....

....

Q2 In one of Gregor Mendel's experiments, he crossed homozygous purple-flowered pea plants with homozygous white-flowered plants. The **first generation** of offspring were **all purple-flowered**.

a) In Mendel's experiment, which characteristic is recessive?

....

b) Using the symbols **F** and **f** to represent the alleles for **purple** and **white**, write down the combination of alleles (genetic make-up) of each of the following:

i) the original purple-flowered parent plant

....

ii) the original white-flowered parent plant

....

iii) the first generation of purple-flowered offspring

....

c) Mendel crossed **two** of the purple flowers from the **first generation** of offspring. What ratio of purple:white flowers would he expect to get? Explain your answer.

....

....

Mixed Questions — Biology 2b

Q3 **Albinism** is a genetic condition. Affected people, called albinos, lack any skin pigmentation. A couple, neither of whom is albino, have a child who is an albino.

Is the allele for albinism dominant or recessive? Explain your answer.

....

....

....

Q4 Two grey rabbits are mated, and eight offspring are produced. Five of the offspring have grey fur, and three have white fur. The allele for grey fur (**G**) is dominant. The allele for white fur (**g**) is recessive. The **parent rabbits** are both have the alleles **Gg**.

a) Draw a **genetic cross diagram** in the space below, to show the **probability** of each combination of alleles occurring in the offspring of the rabbits.

b) **i)** What is the predicted ratio of grey to white rabbits in the offspring?

....

ii) Explain why the actual ratio of colours in the offspring is not exactly the same as this.

....

....

c) If two white rabbits are mated together, what proportion of their offspring will be white? Explain your answer.

....

....

....

Mixed Questions — Biology 2b

Q5 The diagram shows a chalk cliff face and the places where three **fossils** were found in the cliff.

fossil X found here

fossils Y and Z found here

a) The most recent fossil is of a fossilised early fish. Which of the three fossils marked on the diagram is most likely to be the fish fossil?

....

b) Fossils X, Y and Z are all animal fossils. Explain why **animal** fossils are more common than **plant** fossils.

....

....

c) Some scientists have noticed that Fossils Y and Z have a lot of **similar features** and are wondering whether they are both from the same **species**. Explain why is it difficult to find out if they are from the same species just by looking at the fossils.

....

....

Q6 Neela runs a **100 m race**.

a) Describe a **change** that occurred in Neela's circulation system.

....

b) When she finished the race her legs were **tired** and it took a few minutes for her to **catch her breath**.

i) What **process** was producing the **energy** she needed to contract her leg muscles while running?

....

ii) Write the word equation for this process.

....

iii) Why did she have to **continue breathing hard** after she had stopped running?

....

....

c) Neela was hungry after the race, so she ate a sandwich.

i) Which enzyme breaks down the starch from the bread into sugars?

....

ii) Name the **three** places in Neela's body where this enzyme is produced.

....

Mixed Questions — Biology 2b

Q7 Sex determination in chickens is different from in humans. **Male** chickens (cockerels) have **two Z** chromosomes and **females** (hens) have **ZW** chromosomes.

a) What is a chromosome?

....

b) Apart from having different letters, explain how sex determination in chickens differs from humans.

....

Q8 One way that organisms **grow** is by making new cells by **mitosis**.

The graph shows how the amount of DNA per cell changes as a cell undergoes two cell divisions by mitosis. Point C on the graph is the time when the chromosomes first become visible in the new cells.

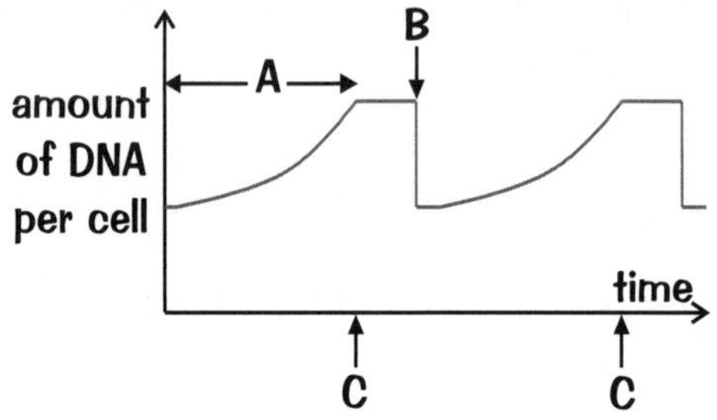

amount of DNA per cell

A

B

time

C

C

a) Describe and explain what is happening to the DNA during stage A.

....

....

b) What happens at time **B**?

....

c) **i)** What type of cells divide by mitosis?

....

ii) What type of reproduction uses mitosis?

....

d) Give **three differences** between mitosis and meiosis.

1. ....

2. ....

3. ....

Osmosis

Q1 This diagram shows a tank separated into two by a partially permeable membrane.

A

B

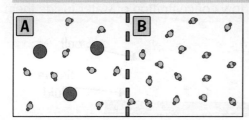

Water molecule

Sucrose molecule

a) On which side of the membrane is there the higher concentration of water molecules?

....

b) In which direction would you expect more water molecules to travel — from A to B or from B to A?

....

c) Predict whether the level of liquid on side B will **rise** or **fall**. Explain your answer.

The liquid level on side B will ...., **because** ....

....

Q2 Some **potato cylinders** were placed in solutions of different **salt concentrations**. At the start of the experiment each cylinder was 50 mm long. Their final lengths are recorded in the table below.

Concentration of salt (molar)	Final length of potato cylinder (mm)	Change in length of potato cylinder (mm)
0	60	
0.25	58	
0.5	56	
0.75	70	
1	50	
1.25	45	

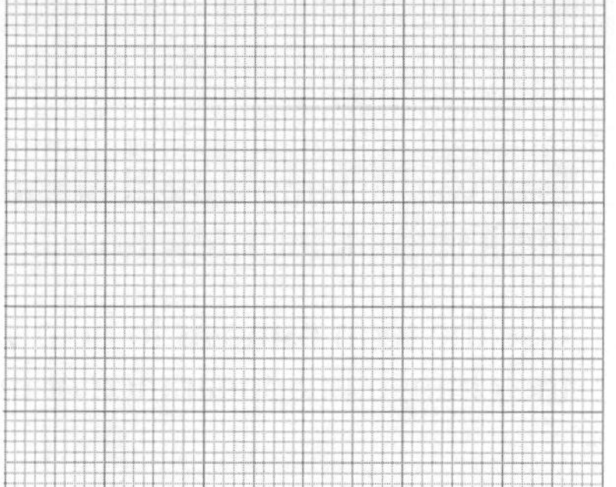

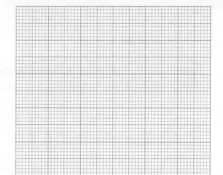

a) Plot the points for concentration of salt solution vs final length of potato cylinders on the grid.

b) Work out the change in length of each of the cylinders and complete the table above.

c) Study the pattern of the results.

i) State the salt concentration(s) that produced unexpected results. ....

ii) Suggest a method for deciding which of the results are correct.

....

d) State three factors that should have been kept constant to ensure this was a fair test.

....

....

....

Osmosis

Q3 The diagram below shows some **body cells** bathed in **tissue fluid**. A blood vessel flows close to the cells, providing water. The cells shown have a low concentration of water inside them.

a) Is the concentration of water higher in the **tissue fluid** or inside the **cells**?

b) In which direction would you expect more water to travel — **into** the cells or **out of** the cells? Explain your answer.

c) Explain why osmosis appears to stop after a while.

Q4 Joan was making a meal of **salted ham** and **fruit salad**. She covered the meat in water and left it to soak for a few hours. When she returned, the meat was much bigger in size.

a) Use the term **osmosis** to help you explain the change in appearance of the ham.

b) To make her fruit salad, Joan cut up some oranges and apples, sprinkled sugar over them and left them overnight. When she examined the fruit next morning it was surrounded by a **liquid**.

i) Suggest what the liquid might be.

ii) Explain where the liquid has come from.

iii) Joan washed some raisins and sultanas to add to her salad. She observed that they became swollen. Explain what has happened this time.

Gas and Solute Exchange

Q1 Substances move through partially permeable membranes by **three** processes.

a) Place a cross in the correct boxes to identify the features of each process.

Feature	Diffusion	Osmosis	Active transport
Substances move from areas of higher concentration to areas of lower concentration			
Requires energy			

b) What is the main difference between diffusion and osmosis?

....

Q2 Indicate whether each of the following statements is **true** or **false**.

	True	False
a) Leaves are adapted to aid the diffusion of gases.	☐	☐
b) Guard cells are important for controlling water loss from leaves.	☐	☐
c) In dry conditions leaf stomata are likely to be open.	☐	☐
d) Air spaces in leaves reduce the surface area for gas exchange.	☐	☐
e) Plants are likely to wilt when they lose more water than is replaced.	☐	☐
f) Plants mainly lose water from their roots.	☐	☐

Q3 A diagram of a cross-section through part of a **leaf** is shown.

a) Suggest what substance is represented by each of the letters shown on the diagram.

A ....

B ....

C ....

b) By what process do all these substances enter and leave the leaf? ....

c) How is the amount of these substances that enter and leave the leaf controlled?

....

....

d) State two places where gaseous exchange takes place in a leaf.

1. ....

2. ....

e) Suggest one advantage of leaves having a flattened shape.

....

Gas and Solute Exchange

Q4 Circle the correct word(s) from each pair to complete the passage below.

In life processes, **gases / solids** and **dissolved / undissolved** substances have to move through an exchange surface to get to where they're needed. Exchange surfaces are adapted to **maximise / minimise** effectiveness. For example, they are **thick / thin** so substances only have a **short / long** distance to diffuse. They have a **small / large** surface area so lots of a substance can diffuse at once. Exchange surfaces in animals have lots of blood vessels to get stuff into and out of the **blood / stomach** quickly. Gas exchange surfaces in animals are often **oily / ventilated** too. Exchanging substances gets more difficult in **smaller / bigger** and more **simple / complex** organisms — the place where the substances are needed is a **short / long** way away from exchange surfaces.

Q5 Lucy was investigating the water loss from basil plants in **different conditions**. She used twelve plants, three plants in each of the four different conditions. The plants were weighed before and after the experiment. She calculated the % change in the mass and recorded her results in a table.

a) Calculate the average % change in plant mass for the three plants in each of the conditions and write the results in the table.

Plant	In a room (% change in mass)	Next to a fan (% change in mass)	By a lamp (% change in mass)	Next to a fan and by a lamp (% change in mass)
1	5	8	10	13
2	5	9	11	15
3	4	11	9	13
Average				

b) Which conditions caused the greatest water loss? Circle the correct answer.

in a room   next to a fan   by a lamp   next to a fan and by a lamp

c) Suggest why Lucy used **three** plants in each of the conditions shown.

....

d) Lucy then covered the lower surfaces of the leaves with **petroleum jelly**. Explain how this would affect the rate of water loss from the leaves.

Petroleum jelly is a waterproof substance.

....

....

e) The water loss from a plant in a hot, dry day is shown on the graph. Sketch the graph you would expect for the same plant on a **cold**, **wet** day.

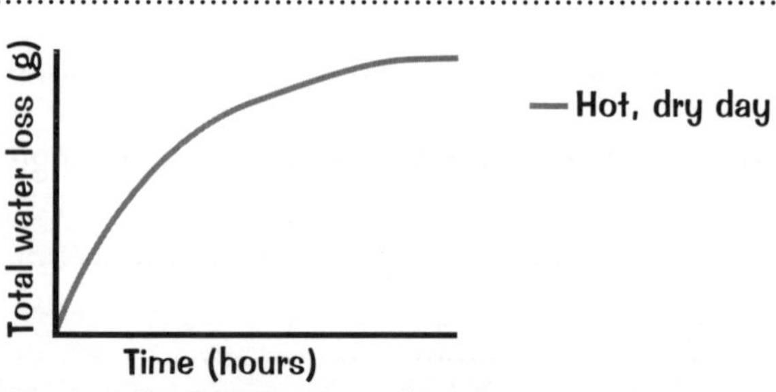

Top Tips: Diffusion, osmosis and active transport... or 'how stuff gets from one place to another' if you like. Remember, active transport is the odd one out — it's **active** so it needs **energy**.

The Breathing System

Q1 **Ventilation** involves the breathing system.

a) Define **ventilation**.

....

b) Explain why ventilation is needed.

....

....

Q2 a) On the diagram show the positions of the following structures by placing the correct letter in the correct box:

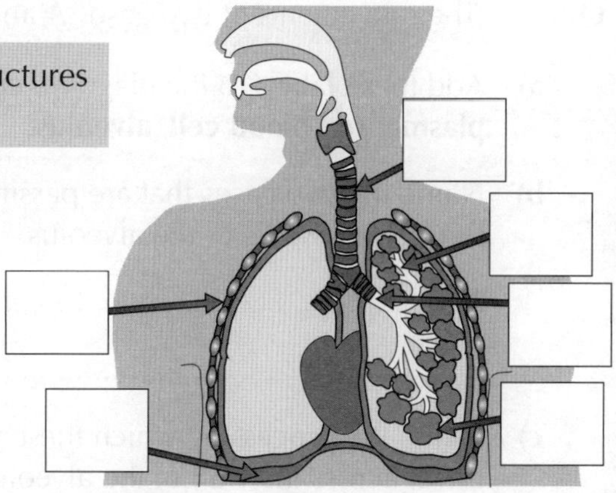

A	alveolus	**D**	bronchiole
B	bronchus	**E**	ribcage
C	trachea	**F**	diaphragm

b) Complete the passages below using the words given. Each word may be used more than once.

out	**flattens**	**drawn into**	**in**		
diaphragm	**increases**	**decreases**	**down**	**intercostal**	**up**
forced out of	**rises**	**volume**	**relax**	**ribcage**	**fall**

i) When we breathe .... the .... muscles and the .... contract. This means the diaphragm .... and the ribcage and the sternum move .... and .... This makes the volume of the thorax .... in size, which causes a .... in pressure. Air is then .... the lungs.

ii) Breathing out occurs when the intercostal muscles and the diaphragm .... This means that the .... and sternum move .... and .... As a result the .... of the thorax .... and the pressure ...., meaning that air is .... the lungs.

Q3 a) What is an **artificial ventilator**?

....

b) Explain how a modern artificial ventilator works.

....

....

Diffusion Through Cell Membranes

Q1 Parts of the human body are **adapted** to speed up the **rate of diffusion** of various substances.

a) State **two** parts of the body that are adapted to aid diffusion.

....

b) Name **two** substances that enter the bloodstream by diffusion.

....

Q2 The movements of two gases **A** and **B** in an **alveolus** are shown.

a) Add these labels to the diagram: **capillary**, **plasma**, **red blood cell**, **alveolus**.

b) Name the two gases that are passing through the walls of the alveolus.

A ....

B ....

c) Name the **process** by which these gases travel across the wall of the alveolus.

....

B

A

Q3 Villi increase the **surface area** of the gut for the uptake of nutrients. Pablo conducted an experiment to investigate the effect of surface area using four **gelatine cubes** of **different sizes**. He placed the cubes in a dish of food dye and measured how quickly they absorbed the dye. His results are shown in the table.

Size (cm)	Surface area (cm^2)	Time taken for dye uptake (s)
1 x 1 x 1		41.6
2 x 2 x 2		9.3
5 x 5 x 5		1.7
10 x 10 x 10		0.4

a) Calculate the missing values for **surface area**.

b) Complete these statements by circling the correct word.

i) As the cubes become bigger in size their surface area becomes **bigger / smaller**.

ii) As the surface area becomes bigger the rate of dye uptake **increases / decreases**.

c) Explain how the results from this experiment show that villi increase the rate of nutrient uptake from the gut.

....

....

d) Give **one** other feature of villi that helps to speed up the uptake of nutrients. ....

Active Transport

Q1 Tick the boxes to show whether the following statements are **true** or **false**.

		True	False
a)	Active transport allows cells to absorb ions from very concentrated solutions.	☐	☐
b)	Active transport allows substances to be taken up against the concentration gradient.	☐	☐
c)	Dissolved substances in the gut move into the blood by active transport.	☐	☐

Q2 A diagram of a **specialised plant cell** is shown.

a) Name the type of cell shown. ....

b) What is the main **function** of this type of cell?

....

c) Explain why minerals are **not** usually absorbed from the soil by the process of **diffusion**.

....

....

d) Explain how these specialised cells absorb minerals from the soil.
Use the words **active transport**, **concentration**, **respiration** and **energy** in your answer.

....

....

Q3 Two germinating barley seedlings were placed in solutions that contained a known concentration of **potassium ions**, as shown in the diagram. The uptake of potassium ions was measured.

a) State **two** ways to ensure this is a fair test.

....

....

The graph below shows the uptake of potassium ions by the barley seedlings.

b) Which curve represents seedling **A**?
Circle the correct answer.

X **Y**

Explain how you decided.

....

....

c) What is the potassium ion uptake for seedling A after **10 minutes**? ....

Water Flow Through Plants

Q1 Complete this diagram of a **plant** according to the instructions given below.

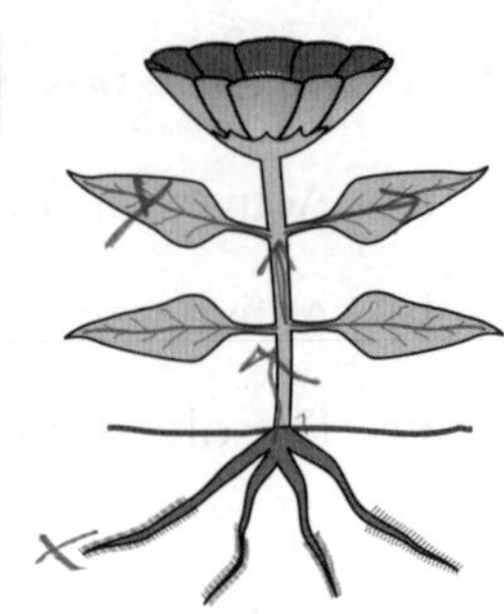

a) Put an **X** on the diagram to show one place where water enters the plant.

b) Add a **Y** to the diagram to show one place where water leaves the plant.

c) Add arrows to the diagram to show how water moves from where it enters to where it leaves.

Q2 Choose from the following words to complete the passage.

Each word can only be used once.

osmosis | leaves | evaporation | roots | flowers | leaf | diffusion | transpiration stream | xylem

Most water leaves plants through the .... by the processes of .... and .... This creates a slight shortage of water in the ...., which draws water from the rest of the plant through the .... vessels. This causes more water to be drawn up from the ...., and so there's a constant .... of water through the plant.

Q3 Flowering plants have **separate transport systems**.

a) Name the **two** types of transport tissue in flowering plants.

1. .... 2. ....

b) i) Which tissue transports water and minerals? ....

ii) Complete the following sentence:

Water and minerals are transported from the .... of the plants to the .... and ....

c) i) Which tissue carries dissolved sugars? ....

ii) Complete the following sentence:

Dissolved sugars are made in the .... and transported to the .... regions and .... organs of plants.

Circulatory System — The Heart

Q1 Tick the boxes to show whether the following statements about the **heart** are **true** or **false**.

	True	False
a) The heart is a tissue.	☐	☑
b) The heart pumps blood around the body.	☑	☐
c) The walls of the heart are mostly made of muscle tissue.	☑	☐
d) The heart has two main chambers.	☐	☑

Q2 The diagram below shows the human **heart**, as seen from the front. The left atrium has been labelled. Complete the remaining labels **a)** to **h)**.

a) pulmonary artery

b) vena cava

c) right atrium

d) right ventricle

e) aorta

f) pulmonary vein

left atrium

g) valves

h) left ventricles

i) What is the function of the valves in the heart and in veins?

prevent back flow of blood

j) Use the words given to fill in the blanks in the paragraph below.

vein heart deoxygenated lungs artery oxygenated ~~double~~

Humans have a ....double.... circulatory system. In the first circuit, blood is pumped from the ....heart.... to the ....lungs.... In the second circuit, ...oxygenated.... blood leaves the heart and goes around to body and ....deoxygenated.... blood returns to the heart.

Top Tips: Make sure that you can label all the bits of the heart and the blood vessels, and that you understand exactly where the blood goes. Remember, **a**rteries carry blood **a**way from the heart.

Circulatory System — The Heart

Q3 State two **functions** of the circulation system. For each function you have given name **two substances** that are **transported**.

Function 1: ....

substances transported: .... and ....

Function 2: ....

substances transported: .... and ....

Q4 Put the words below in the boxes to show the correct sequence of **blood flow** around the body. Each word may be used more than once. The first one has been done for you.

arteries **ventricles** **atria** **veins** **out** **organs**

Blood enters the ....atria......... of the heart.

The ...atria............ contract and force blood into the ...ventricles...

The ..ventricles...... contract and force blood ......out............ of the heart.

Blood flows from the heart to ....organs..... through ....arteries.......

Blood returns to the heart through ....veins.........

Q5 The diagram shows the **blood vessels** of the **heart**.

Write the name of each blood vessel beside the letters on the diagram.

A ..pulmonary artery

B ..aorta..............................

C ....vena cava..................

D ..pulmonary vein.......

Right-hand side

Left-hand side

Circulatory System — Blood Vessels

Q1 A diagram of a **capillary** is shown.

a) Capillary walls are only **one cell** thick.
How does this feature make them suited to their function?

b) Name **two gases** that diffuse through the walls of capillaries.

c) Name **one** other substance that diffuses through the walls of capillaries.

Q2 The pictures below show cross sections of two **blood vessels** — an artery and a vein.

a) Which blood vessel is an artery and which a vein?

A = ... B = ...

b) Explain how the following structures are related to the **function** of the blood vessel.

i) Muscular and elastic walls of arteries

ii) Valves in veins

Q3 Gareth did an experiment to compare the elasticity of **arteries** and **veins**. He dissected out an artery and a vein from a piece of fresh meat. He then took a 5 cm length of each vessel, hung different masses on it, and measured how much it stretched. His results are shown in the table.

mass added (g)	length of blood vessel (mm)	
	artery	vein
0	50	50
5	51	53
10	53	56
15	55	59
20	56	-

a) Suggest one way in which Gareth could tell which was the artery and which was the vein when he was dissecting the meat.

b) If Gareth plots his results on a graph, which variable should he put on the vertical axis, and why?

c) Which vessel stretched more easily? Explain why this was.

d) Why did he take both vessels from the same piece of meat?

Circulatory System — The Blood

Q1 Which of these statements are **true**, and which are **false**? Tick the correct boxes.

		True	False
a)	The function of red blood cells is to fight germs.		✓
b)	White blood cells have no nucleus.		✓
c)	The liquid part of blood is called urine.		✓
d)	Platelets are small fragments of cells.	✓	
e)	Platelets help seal wounds to prevent blood loss.	✓	
f)	Platelets have a nucleus.		✓
g)	Blood is a tissue.	✓	

Tissues are made of groups of similar cells.

Q2 **Red blood cells** carry **oxygen** in the blood.

a) i) Name the substance in red blood cells that combines with oxygen. haemoglobin

ii) Name the substance created when oxygen joins with this substance. oxyhaemoglobin

b) Red blood cells are replaced about every 120 days. Approximately how many times per year are all the red cells in the body replaced? ....

Q3 **White blood cells** defend the body against **disease**.

State three ways in which white blood cells can protect your body from microorganisms.

1. ....

2. ....

3. ....

Q4 a) List six things that are carried by **plasma**.

1. .... 4. ....

2. .... 5. ....

3. .... 6. ....

b) For each of the substances listed in the table, state where each is travelling **from** and **to** in the blood.

Substance	Travelling from	Travelling to
Urea		
Carbon dioxide		
Glucose		

Circulation Aids

Q1 Complete the passage using the words provided below.

heart attack **narrow** **beating** **irritate** **open** **tubes**
clotting **muscles** **arteries** **scar tissue** **coronary**

Stents are .... that can be inserted inside coronary .... that have become too .... Stents keep them ...., making sure blood can pass through to the heart .... This keeps the person's heart .... Stents are a way of lowering the risk of a .... in a person with .... heart disease. But over time, the artery can narrow again as stents can .... the artery and make .... grow. The patient also has to take drugs to stop blood .... on the stent.

Q2 Read the descriptions of the following patients before choosing a suitable treatment (A, B, C or D) from the list.

A — artificial heart transplant

B — artificial replacement valve

C — artificial blood product

D — stent

a) Annie has been involved in an accident and has lost a lot of blood. ☐

b) Alistair has been diagnosed with a blocked artery to the heart muscle. ☐

c) Clive has a damaged heart valve. He is known to react badly to the drugs that are normally used to suppress the immune system. ☐

d) Valerie is a 40 year old woman, who has a badly diseased heart. She is in danger of dying very soon if she is not treated. ☐

Q3 Artificial hearts are mechanical devices that can pump a person's blood if their heart fails.

a) Other than keeping them alive, give **one** advantage to a patient of receiving an artificial heart.

....

b) Give **two** disadvantages to a patient of receiving an artificial heart.

....

....

Top Tips: You might be asked to evaluate artificial replacements in your exam — don't panic, look at any information given and use your knowledge of the pros and cons to write your answer.

Homeostasis

Q1 Define the word '**homeostasis**'.

....

Q2 **Waste products** have to be removed from the body.

a) How is carbon dioxide removed from the body?

....

b) Other than carbon dioxide, name one waste product that the body needs to remove.

....

Q3 The human body needs to be kept at a temperature of around **37 °C**.

a) Explain how your body **monitors** its internal temperature.

....

....

b) How does the body receive information about skin temperature?

....

Q4 a) Fill in this table describing how different parts of the body help to bring your body temperature back to normal if you get **too hot** or **too cold**. One has been done for you.

	Too hot	Too cold
hair	**Hairs lie down flat**	
sweat glands		
blood vessels		

b) Describe how **shivering** helps to warm the body when it's cold.

....

....

The Kidneys and Homeostasis

Q1 Tick the correct boxes to show whether these sentences are **true** or **false**.

		True	False
a)	The kidneys make urea.	☐	☐
b)	Breaking down excess amino acids produces urea.	☐	☐
c)	The liver makes urea.	☐	☐
d)	The kidneys monitor blood temperature.	☐	☐
e)	The bladder stores urine.	☐	☐

Q2 One of the kidney's roles is to adjust the **ion content** of the **blood**.

a) Where do the ions in the body come from?

....

b) What would happen if the ion content of the blood wasn't controlled?

....

....

Q3 The kidneys are involved in the control of the body's **water levels**.

Complete the table showing how your body maintains a water balance on hot and cold days.

	Do you sweat **a lot** or **a little**?	Is the amount of urine you produce **high** or **low**?	Is the urine you produce **more** or **less** concentrated?
Hot Day			
Cold Day			

Q4 You can replace lost water during exercise by consuming a **sports drink**.

a) i) Apart from water, name **two** substances that sports drinks usually contain.

1. .... 2. ....

ii) For each of the substances you named in part **a) i)**, explain their function in a sports drink.

....

....

b) Some sports drink manufacturers claim that their drink will rehydrate you faster than water. Suggest **one** thing you need to look out for when deciding whether the claim is true or not.

....

Kidney Function

Q1 The diagram shows the steps that occur from the entry of blood into the kidneys to the exit of blood from the kidneys. Write the labels **A** to **G** in the diagram to show the correct order.

A Wastes such as urea, are carried out of the nephron to the bladder, whilst reabsorbed materials leave the kidneys in the renal vein.

B Small molecules are squeezed into the Bowman's capsule. Large molecules remain in the blood.

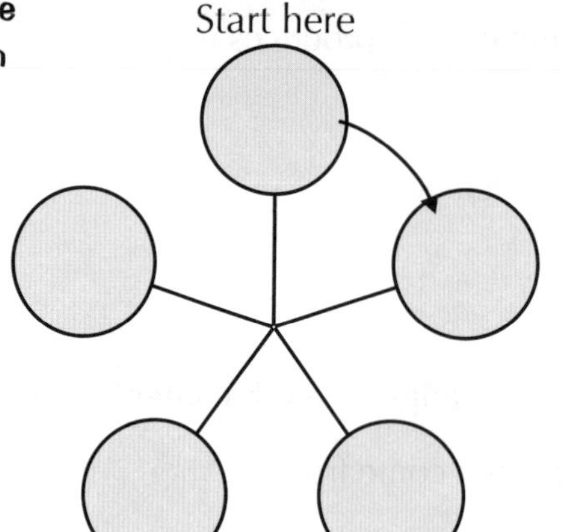

C Useful products are reabsorbed from the nephron and enter the capillaries.

D Molecules travel from the Bowman's capsule along the nephron.

E Blood enters the kidney through the renal artery.

Q2 The blood entering the kidney contains the following:

ions **water** **proteins** **sugar** **urea** **blood cells**

a) List the things that are:

i) filtered out of the blood ....

ii) reabsorbed ....

iii) released in the urine ....

b) Which process is responsible for the **reabsorption** of each substance you have listed above?

....

c) **i)** Name two things that do **not** enter the Bowman's capsule.

....

ii) Explain why these things are not able to leave the bloodstream.

....

Q3 Three people are tested to see how healthy their kidneys are. Levels of **protein** and **glucose** in their urine are measured. The results are shown in the table.

Which of the three subjects might have kidney damage? Explain how you decided.

....

....

....

Subject	Protein (mg/24 hours)	Glucose (mmol/litre)
1	12	0
2	260	1.0
3	0	0

Kidney Failure

Q1 **Kidney failure** can be treated by dialysis or a kidney transplant.
Place a tick in the table to show the features of the two types of treatment.

Feature of treatment	Dialysis	Transplant
High risk of infection		
Long-term, one-off treatment		
Patient can lead a relatively normal life		
Patient must take drugs		
Patient usually needs to live near a hospital		

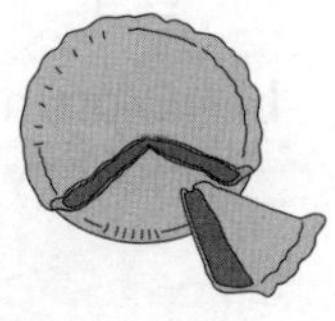

Q2 A model of **dialysis** is shown below. No movement of substances has taken place yet.

Blood | Dialysis fluid

membrane

Red blood cell
Protein
Urea
Water
Glucose

a) i) Which two substances will **not** diffuse across the membrane from the bloodstream into the dialysis fluid.

....

ii) Explain your answer.

....

....

b) Which substance's concentration will increase in the dialysis fluid? ....

c) What do you notice about the concentration of glucose on either side of the membrane? Suggest a reason for this.

....

....

Q3 A donor kidney can be **rejected** by a patient's immune system.

a) Explain why a patient's antibodies may attack the antigens on a donor kidney.

....

b) List **two** steps that are taken to reduce the chances of rejection of a transplanted kidney.

1. ....

2. ....

Kidney Failure

Q4 One method of treatment for kidney failure is to use **dialysis**.

a) The steps in dialysis are listed. Number the steps in the correct order by writing 1 to 5 in the boxes.

- ☐ Excess water, ions and wastes are filtered out of the blood and pass into the dialysis fluid.
- ☐ The patient's blood flows into the dialysis machine and between partially permeable membranes that are surrounded by dialysis fluid.
- ☐ Blood is returned to the patient's body using a vein in their arm.
- ☐ Dialysis continues until nearly all the waste and excess substances are removed.
- ☐ A needle is inserted into a blood vessel in the patient's arm to remove blood.

b) Explain why it is important that the dialysis fluid has the same concentration of dissolved ions as healthy blood.

....

c) Why does dialysis need to be done regularly?

....

Q5 The table shows the number of UK patients with **kidney failure** in **2004** and predicted numbers for **2013**.

a) Calculate the number of patients who received a kidney **transplant** in **2004**. Write your answer in the table.

b) Calculate the number of patients who are likely to be receiving **dialysis** in **2013**. Write your answer in the table.

	Year	
	2004	**2013**
Total number of patients with kidney failure	37 000	68 000
Number receiving dialysis	20 500	
Number that have received a transplant		30 000

c) This table shows the cost of each treatment.

Calculate the amount of money saved per patient when a **transplant** is performed:

Treatment	Average cost per patient (£)
Dialysis	30 000 per year
Transplant	20 000
Anti-rejection drugs	6 500 per year

i) instead of **one** year of **dialysis**.

....

ii) instead of **three** years of **dialysis**.

....

....

Don't forget that transplant patients need drugs to stop organ rejection.

Top Tips: Kidneys do loads of important jobs and that's why kidney failure is so dangerous. You can live with only one kidney though — so it's possible for some people with kidney failure to receive a donated kidney from a member of their family or from another suitable donor.

Controlling Blood Glucose

Q1 Most people's **blood sugar** level is controlled as part of **homeostasis**.

a) Where does the **sugar** in your blood come from?

....

b) Name **one organ** that is involved in the control of blood sugar level.

....

c) Name **two hormones** involved in the regulation of blood sugar level.

....

Q2 Complete the flow chart to show what happens when the **glucose** level in the blood gets too **high**.

Blood contains too much glucose.

↓

.... is released by the ....

↓

.... makes the .... store glucose. Excess blood glucose is converted to ....

↓

.... is removed from the ....

↓

Blood glucose level is now ....

Q3 Explain how the blood sugar level is controlled when there is **not enough** glucose in the blood.

....

....

....

Controlling Blood Glucose

Q4 Ruby and Paul both have **type 1 diabetes**, so they need to **control** their glucose levels carefully.

a) Explain what type 1 diabetes is.

....

....

b) Describe **three** ways that diabetics can **control** their blood sugar levels.

1. ....

2. ....

3. ....

Q5 A lot of **research** is being done by scientists into the **treatment** of diabetes.

a) **i)** Describe a major improvement that has been made to the **source** of the insulin used by diabetics.

....

....

ii) What is the main advantage of using this new source of insulin?

....

b) **i)** What **surgical** treatment can be used to cure type 1 diabetes?

....

ii) Describe **two problems** with the treatment you have named.

....

....

c) Scientists are constantly researching new treatments and cures for diabetes.
Name **two** treatments that are currently in development.

1. ....

2. ....

Top Tips: Although diabetes is a serious disease, many diabetics are able to control their blood sugar levels and carry on with normal lives. Sir Steve Redgrave even won a gold medal at the Olympics after he had been diagnosed with type 1 diabetes.

Mixed Questions — Biology 3a

Q1 We each have around 600 million **alveoli** in our lungs. This ensures that we can get enough oxygen into our bloodstream and remove the waste carbon dioxide from it.

a) Describe **four** ways in which the alveoli are specialised to maximise gas exchange.

....

....

....

....

b) i) Which **cells** in the blood carry the oxygen that has diffused through the alveoli walls?

....

ii) Which **substance** in the cell combines with the oxygen? ....

iii) How are the cells **adapted** to carry oxygen?

....

....

Q2 The diagram shows a **specialised cell**.

a) Name the cell shown.

....

b) Explain how the cell's **shape** helps it to absorb **water**.

....

c) The cell is exposed to a poison that stops respiration. Why would this affect the uptake of **minerals** but not the uptake of **water**?

....

....

d) i) Water absorbed by the roots is lost through the leaves as vapour. What process does it escape by?

....

ii) Under what conditions is water loss at its greatest? ....

iii) Name another gas that escapes out of a leaf. ....

Human Impact on the Environment

Q1 Circle the correct word to complete each sentence below.

a) The size of the human population now is **bigger** / **smaller** than it was 1000 years ago.

b) The growth of the human population now is **slower** / **faster** than it was 1000 years ago.

c) The human impact on the environment now is **less** / **greater** than it was 1000 years ago.

Q2 One way to assess a person's impact on the Earth is to use an **ecological footprint**. This involves calculating **how many Earths** would be needed if everyone lived like that person. It takes into account things like the amount of **waste** the person produces and how much **energy** they use.

a) Two men calculate their ecological footprints. Eight Earths would be needed to support everyone in the way John lives. Half an Earth would be enough to support everyone in the way Derek lives.

i) One of the men lives in a UK city, and one in rural Kenya. Who is more likely to live where?

....

ii) Tick any of the following that are possible reasons for the difference in results.

☐ John buys more belongings, which use more raw materials to manufacture.

☐ John has central heating in his home but Derek has a wood fire.

☐ John throws away less waste.

☐ John drives a car and Derek rides a bicycle.

b) Suggest one thing John could do to reduce the size of his ecological footprint.

....

Q3 Some water voles have been nesting in an area of marsh land. A farmer wants to **drain** half of the marsh to grow crops.

a) i) State whether you would expect the population of voles to increase or decrease.

....

ii) Give **one** reason for your answer to part **i)**.

....

....

b) Name **two** human activities, apart from farming, that reduce the amount of land available for animals and plants.

1. ....

2. ....

Human Impact on the Environment

Q4 The size of the Earth's **population** has an impact on our **environment**.

a) Use the table below to plot a graph on the grid, showing how the world's human population has changed over the last 1000 years.

NO. OF PEOPLE (BILLIONS)	YEAR
0.3	1000
0.4	1200
0.4	1400
0.6	1600
1.0	1800
1.7	1900
6.1	2000

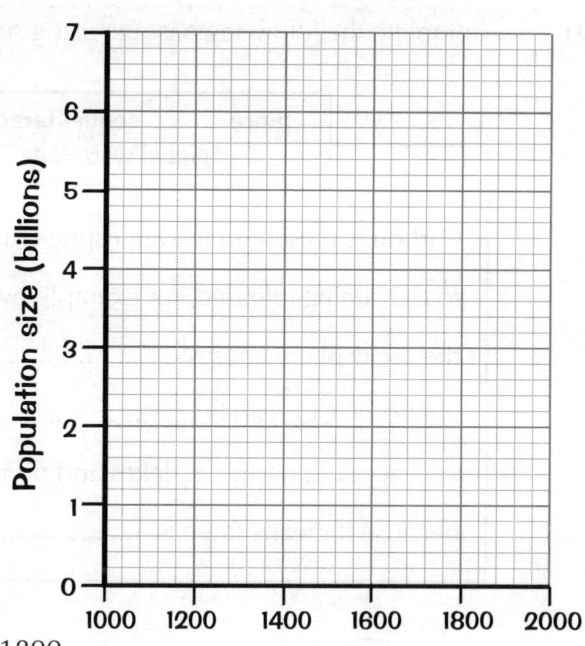

b) Suggest two reasons for the sudden increase after 1800.

....

....

c) What effect is an increasing population having on the amount of waste we produce?

....

Q5 As the human population **grows** we need more **food**. Modern farming methods can increase the amount of food grown, but they may harm the environment.

a) Give three types of chemicals used in modern farming.

1. ....

2. ....

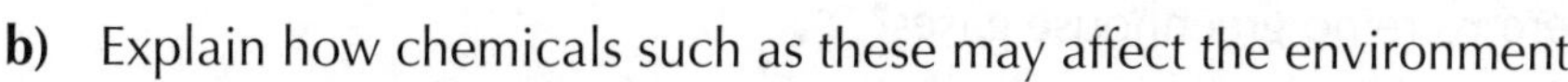

3. ....

b) Explain how chemicals such as these may affect the environment.

....

....

....

Top Tips: There's lots to think about with this topic. It's the kind of thing you might get a longer answer question on in an exam, where you have to weigh up all the different arguments. And examiners can't get enough of that graph where the human population goes shooting up — they love it.

Carbon Dioxide and the Greenhouse Effect

Q1 Complete the following passage using some of the words from the list below.

more sequestered oceans less burning
global warming carbon dioxide making

Carbon is present in the atmosphere as .... (CO_2). Lots of processes lead to CO_2 being released, for example by .... fossil fuels. Too much CO_2 in the atmosphere causes ....

However, CO_2 can be .... ('locked up') in natural stores, including ...., lakes and ponds. Storing CO_2 in these ways is really important because it means there is .... CO_2 in the atmosphere.

Q2 Underline the statements below about the greenhouse effect that are **true**.

The greenhouse effect is needed for life on Earth as we know it.

Greenhouse gases include carbon dioxide and sulfur dioxide.

The greenhouse effect causes acid rain.

Increasing amounts of greenhouse gases is causing global warming.

Q3 The Earth receives energy from the **Sun**. It radiates much of this energy back towards space.

a) Explain the role of the greenhouse gases in keeping the Earth warm.

....

....

....

b) What would happen if there were no greenhouse gases?

....

....

c) In recent years the amounts of greenhouse gases in the atmosphere have increased.
Explain how this leads to global warming.

....

....

Deforestation and the Destruction of Peat Bogs

Q1 **Deforestation** means **cutting down** forests. It can lead to big environmental problems.

a) Explain how deforestation leads to an increase in the amount of carbon dioxide in the atmosphere.

....

....

....

....

b) Some forest is cleared to provide land for farming.
Tick the boxes to show whether these statements are true or false.

	True	False
i) Rearing cattle decreases the amount of methane released into the atmosphere.	☐	☐
ii) Rice is grown in warm, waterlogged conditions that are ideal for decomposers. Decomposers produce methane.	☐	☐

c) Give **two** reasons, apart from creating more farmland, why humans cut forests down.

....

....

Q2 **Ecosystems** like rainforests contain many different **species**. If we destroy rainforests we risk making species extinct and **reducing biodiversity**.

a) Define the term '**biodiversity**'.

....

b) Describe **one** implication for humans of reducing biodiversity.

....

Q3 The destruction of **peat bogs** releases **carbon dioxide** into the atmosphere.

a) Briefly describe how peat is formed.

....

....

b) Explain why draining a peat bog increases the level of carbon dioxide in the atmosphere.

....

....

c) Suggest **one** thing that a **gardener** could do to help reduce the number of peat bogs being drained.

....

Climate Change

Q1 These statements help explain how **global warming** may lead to floods. Use them to complete the **flow chart** below, which has one box filled in to start you off.

Low-lying areas are at risk of flooding. **Higher temperatures make ice melt.**

Sea levels start to rise.

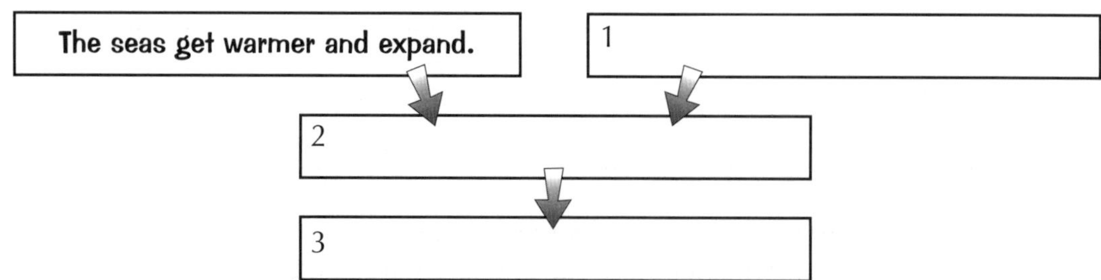

Q2 Circle the correct words to complete the sentences about **global warming** below.

a) Global warming could **increase** / **reduce** biodiversity.

b) As northern areas get warmer, some birds might migrate further **north** / **south**.

c) Species that need **warmer** / **cooler** temperatures to survive may become **more** / **less** widely distributed as the conditions they thrive in exist over a smaller area.

d) Global warming may change weather patterns across the world, leading to more **mild** / **extreme** weather in many places.

Q3 Two university students carried out **observations**. Student A noticed that a glacier was melting. Student B noticed that daffodils were flowering earlier in 2006 than in 2005. Both students concluded that this was due to **global warming**. Are they right? Explain your answer.

....

....

Q4 There's a **scientific consensus** that global warming is happening. This means scientists have collected enough **evidence** to accept the **hypothesis**.

a) What is meant by evidence and hypothesis?

evidence: ....

hypothesis: ....

b) Give examples of the sort of data that scientists are collecting about climate change.

....

....

Biofuels

Q1 In the sentences below, circle the correct word.

a) Fermentation is a form of **digestion** / **respiration**.

b) Fermentation is **aerobic** / **anaerobic**.

c) Fermentation by yeast produces **ethanol** / **methane**.

d) **Ethanol** / **Biogas** can be mixed with petrol and used to fuel cars — this is known as gasohol.

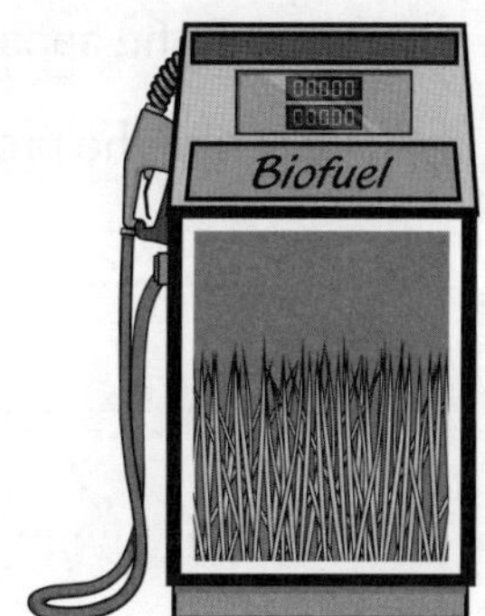

Q2 **Ethanol** is a biofuel that can be made from specially grown crops. Fill in the gaps in the sentences below about ethanol.

a) Ethanol is made by fermenting sugar, such as ....

b) The sugar is extracted from crops, such as ....

Q3 Use the words below to fill in the gaps and complete the passage about **biogas**.

batch	generator	fermented	heating	turbine	waste	carbohydrates

Biogas can be made in a container called a ...., either by continuous production or by .... production. It is made from plant and animal .... which contains .... and is .... by microorganisms.

Biogas could be used for ...., or even to power a .... for making electricity.

Q4 Below are some fairly straightforward questions about **biogas**. Great.

a) Name the main components of biogas.

....

b) Name **two** materials that might be used as food for the microorganisms used in producing biogas.

....

....

Using Biogas Generators

Q1 Kapilisha did an experiment to produce **biogas** in the laboratory. After setting up the experiment, she left the apparatus in a warm place for five weeks. The diagram below shows her apparatus.

rubber tube
balloon
plastic bottle
one-way valve
biomass mixed with distilled water

a) Describe the process going on inside the plastic bottle.

....

....

....

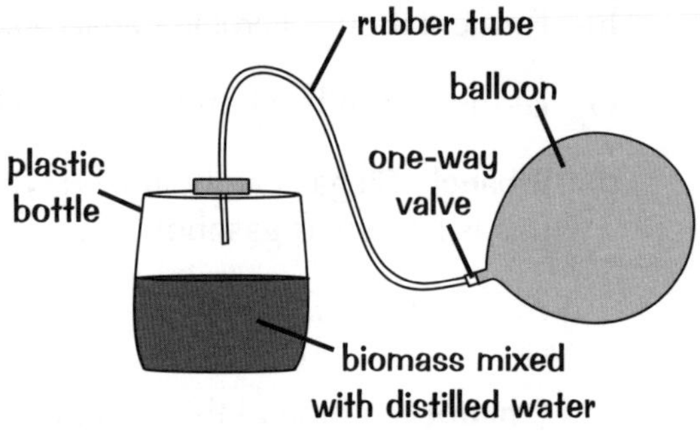

b) If biogas was produced, what change would be visible after a few weeks?

....

c) Explain why the bottle was left in a **warm** place during the five weeks.

....

....

Q2 Professor Wiggins did an experiment to find the best **temperature** for **biogas production**. The graph below shows what she found.

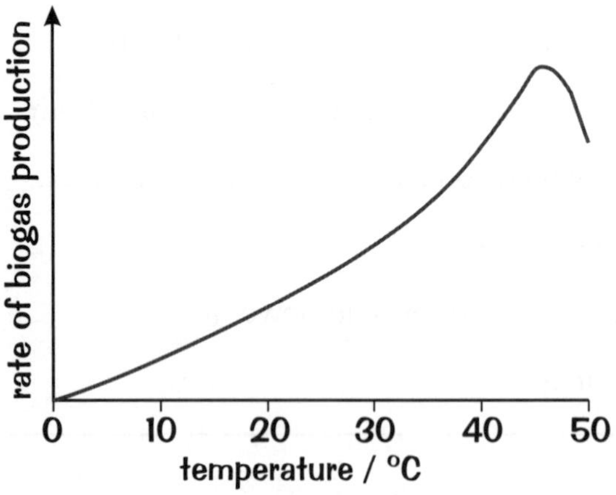

rate of biogas production
0 10 20 30 40 50
temperature / °C

a) What is the best temperature for biogas production? ....

b) Professor Wiggins decided to set up her biogas generator at a temperature **slightly below** the best temperature. Suggest a reason for this.

....

....

....

c) Suggest **two** variables apart from temperature that might also affect the rate of biogas production.

....

....

d) Sewage can be used for biogas production, but it is important that the sewage contains as few chemical toxins as possible. Explain why this is important.

....

....

Using Biogas Generators

Q3 Biogas may be produced in a **batch** or **continuous** generator from waste materials, e.g. animal waste. Circle the correct words below to describe how a batch and continuous generator differ.

a) In a **batch / continuous** generator, waste is usually loaded manually.

b) A **batch / continuous** generator is the best choice for large-scale production.

c) In a continuous generator, waste is added **at intervals / all the time**.

d) In a **batch / continuous** generator, biogas is produced at a steady rate.

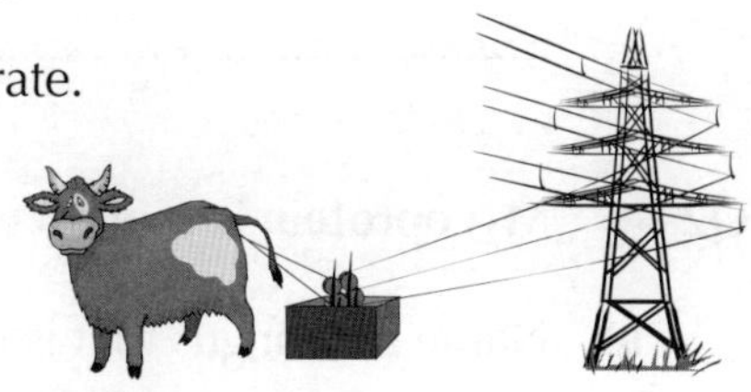

Q4 In a village in South America, a **biogas generator** was built.

a) Suggest reasons for the following features of the design:

i) The generator was built some distance away from houses in the village.

....

ii) The generator was built close to fields where animals were grazing.

....

iii) The generator was covered with insulating material.

....

b) Describe **two** possible advantages for the villagers in having a biogas generator like this.

....

....

Q5 The diagram on the right shows a **biogas generator system**.

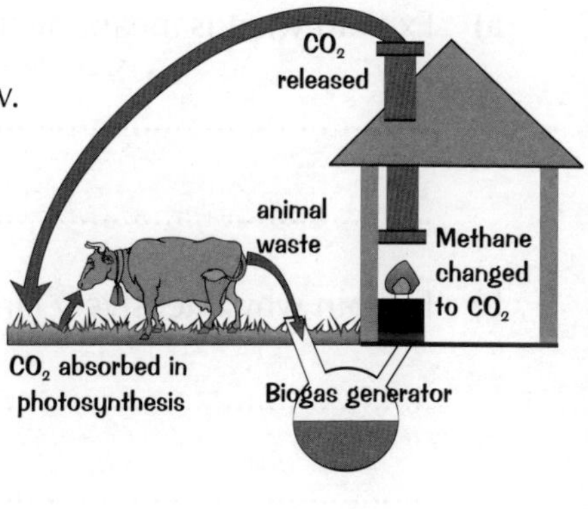

a) The energy in biogas originally came from the **Sun**. Explain how.

....

....

....

b) Biogas is sometimes described as being '**carbon neutral**'.

i) Explain why biogas is carbon neutral.

....

....

ii) Name **two other** reasons why biogas is less damaging to the environment than many fuels.

....

....

Managing Food Production

Q1 Three different **food chains** are shown here.

Grass → Cattle → Human

Pondweed → Small fish → Salmon → Human

Wheat → Human

a) Circle the food chain that shows the most **efficient** production of **food** for **humans**.

b) Explain your choice.

....

Q2 **Mycoprotein** is used to make protein-rich **meat substitutes** for vegetarian meals.

a) Name the fungus that is used to produce mycoprotein.

....

b) Complete this passage about making mycoprotein using some of the words from the list below.

oxygen	purified	vegetable oil	fermenters
recycled	carbon dioxide	glucose syrup	

The fungus is grown in ...., using .... as food. The fungus respires aerobically, so .... is supplied, together with nitrogen and other minerals. When enough mycoprotein has grown, it is harvested and then ....

Q3 In the UK a lot of our pork comes from **intensively farmed** pigs.

a) Explain what is meant by 'intensive farming'.

....

....

b) Explain why intensively farming pigs makes pork production more efficient.

....

....

....

c) Give one benefit to the consumer of farming pigs intensively.

....

Top Tips: Energy and biomass are lost every time you move up a stage in a food chain. So reducing the number of stages in a food chain increases the efficiency of food production.

Problems With Food Production and Distribution

Q1 The structure of the UK **egg industry** has changed in recent years. The table below shows the percentages of the egg market represented by three methods of chicken farming — **laying** (battery hens), **barn** (hens that roam freely indoors) and **free range** (hens that roam freely outdoors).

	Percentage of egg market for each type of chicken farming		
Year	Laying	Barn	Free range
1999	78	6	16
2001	72	5	23
2003	69	6	25
2005	66	7	27
Change			

a) Use this data to make a bar chart on the grid above.

b) Calculate the change in the percentage of the market held by each farming type between 1999 and 2005. Write your answers in the spaces on the table.

final % – initial %

c) Suggest a reason for the changes.

....

....

Q2 Explain why products that have lots of '**food miles**' can be bad for the **environment**.

....

....

....

Q3 **Overfishing** has caused a large fall in the number of fish in our oceans.

a) Explain how **fishing quotas** can help to maintain fish stocks.

....

....

b) Continuing to fish, whilst maintaining fish stocks at a level where the fish can still breed, is an example of **sustainable food production**.
What is meant by 'sustainable food production'?

....

....

Mixed Questions — Biology 3b

Q1 **Intensive farming** is one way of making food production more **efficient**.

a) Circle the correct words to complete the sentences below about the problems of intensive farming.

i) The **warm / crowded** conditions make it **easy / hard** for diseases to spread.

ii) The animals are frequently given **pesticides / antibiotics**, which get into the human food chain.

iii) Heating the animal buildings **increases / decreases** a farm's energy use.

b) Martin intensively farms turkeys. He wants to use the turkeys' waste to produce energy.
Name a fuel that Martin could make using the animal waste.

....

Q2 The graph below shows changes in **global temperature** since 1859.

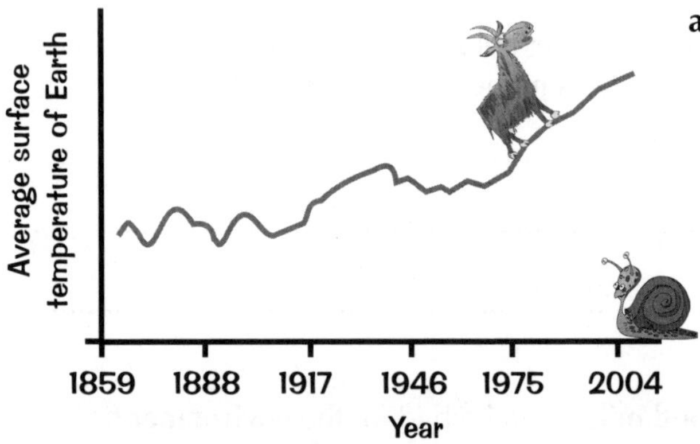

a) Describe the trend shown on the graph.

....

....

....

b) The next graph shows how current levels of three gases compare to their levels before the Industrial Revolution.

Change in atmospheric concentration (%)
pre-industrial level (100%)
CO_2
methane
nitrous oxide

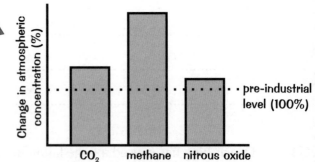

i) Which gas has had the biggest percentage increase in concentration?

....

ii) Give one source of this gas.

....

c) What conclusion can you draw from these two graphs?
Did one of the changes definitely cause the other?

....

....

....

Answers

Contents

Biology 1a — Human Biology

Biology 1a — Human Biology

Pages 1-2 — Diet and Metabolic Rate

Q1 A diet containing the right balance of different foods and the right amount of energy.

Q2 a) Protein is needed for **growth** and **cell repair/replacement** (in either order).

b) Carbohydrates provide much of your **energy**.

c) Fats are needed to **keep warm** and for **energy** (in either order). Other answers are possible.

d) Vitamins and minerals are needed in **tiny/small** amounts to stay healthy.

Q3 a) The speed at which all the chemical reactions that take place in your body happen.

b) proportion of muscle to fat in the body, inherited factors, amount of exercise

Q4 Wendy needs more carbohydrate and protein in her diet because she is more physically active. She needs more protein for muscle development and more carbohydrate for energy.

Q5 a) The average man is bigger than the average woman and so needs more energy for metabolic reactions and movement. The average man also has more muscle, which needs more energy than fatty tissue.

b) Cyclists riding in the Tour de France are doing a lot of exercise every day, and active people need more energy. They may also be more muscular than the average man.

Q6 a) Egg

b) In 50 g of bread there are $(50 \div 100) \times 60 = 30$ g carbs.
In 50 g of milk there are $(50 \div 100) \times 10 = 5$ g carbs.
$30 - 5 = 25$ g more carbohydrate in the bread.

c) Any fruit or vegetable. This would provide vitamins, minerals and fibre.

Page 3 — Factors Affecting Health

Q1 a) They have an unbalanced diet.

b) A disease caused by a lack of vitamins or minerals.

Q2 You will be 'fit' if you take regular exercise, but if your diet isn't balanced or you're lacking in a certain nutrient, you will be malnourished.

Q3 a) $(16 \div 50) \times 100 = 32\%$.

b) E.g. bad diet, overeating and not enough exercise.

c) Heart disease, cancers and type 2 diabetes should be underlined.

Q4 a) E.g. exercise increases the amount of energy used by the body and decreases the amount stored as fat.
So people who exercise are less likely to suffer from health problems like obesity.

b) E.g. inherited factors can affect a person's metabolic rate or cholesterol level.

Page 4 — Evaluating Food, Lifestyle and Diet

Q1 less, use, less, increases

Q2 Report B is likely to be more reliable as it was published in a reputable journal, probably conducted by an independent researcher, and used a large sample size.

Q3 a) Burger B is the most unhealthy because it contains a higher proportion of fat (including saturated fat) and carbohydrate than Burger A, and has a higher energy content.

b) Sharon's lifestyle could increase her risk of obesity. This is because she's taking in a lot of energy by eating Burger B regularly, but not using much energy because she doesn't exercise.

Pages 5-6 — Fighting Disease

Q1 A microorganism that causes infectious disease.

Q2 A molecule that causes an immune response.

Q3 a) true

b) false

c) false

d) false

e) true

Q4 small, damaging, toxins, poisons, cells, copies, bursts, damage

Q5 a) Blood clots are used to quickly seal the skin if it's damaged and keep microorganisms out.

b) The air passages are lined with mucus and cilia to trap and remove the bacteria before they reach the lungs.

Q6 a) White blood cells can engulf and digest microbes. They produce antibodies to kill invading cells, and also antitoxins to neutralise any toxins they produce.

b) No — a different antibody is needed to recognise each different species of microorganism.

Q7 If a person is infected with chickenpox again their white blood cells will rapidly produce the antibodies to kill it. So they are naturally immune to chickenpox and won't get ill.

Pages 7-8 — Fighting Disease — Vaccination

Q1 causing damage, will

Q2 a) i) true

ii) true

iii) false

iv) true

b) Dead and inactive microorganisms are harmless but the body will still produce antibodies to attack them.

Q3 The children who did not get the disease were in better general health.

Q4 John is protected from infection because his white blood cells can make antibodies to the virus a lot quicker than James's can. When John was vaccinated, he was given some inactive tuberculosis (TB) pathogens. These had antigens on the surface. John's white blood cells then learnt to make the antibodies specific to these antigens.

Q5 a) measles, mumps and rubella

b) E.g. the risk of catching the diseases decreases if more children are vaccinated.

Q6 a) They've helped to control lots of infectious diseases that were once common in the UK, so far fewer people catch diseases like polio, whooping cough, measles, rubella, mumps or tetanus.

b) Any two of, e.g. Some people do not become immune after vaccination. / Others can experience a bad reaction, e.g. swelling at the injection site. / In rare cases there could even be a serious reaction such as seizures.

Pages 9-10 — Fighting Disease — Drugs

Q1 a) The medicine doesn't kill the virus causing the cold — it just relieves the symptoms.

b) Colds are caused by a virus and antibiotics only kill bacteria.

c) Because viruses reproduce using your own body cells, which makes it very difficult to develop drugs that destroy just the virus without killing the body's cells.

d) Different antibiotics kill different types of bacteria, so a patient needs to be treated with the right antibiotic for it to have an effect.

Q2 a) 9 days

b) Because doctors usually only prescribe antibiotics for something more serious than a sore throat (to avoid over-prescribing antibiotics).

Q3 a)
1. Bacteria mutate and sometimes the mutations cause them to be resistant to an antibiotic.
2. So if you have an infection, some of the bacteria might be resistant to antibiotics.
3. When you treat the infection, only the non-resistant strains of bacteria will be killed.
4. The individual resistant bacteria will survive and reproduce.
5. The population of the resistant strain of bacteria will increase.

b) E.g. MRSA

Biology 1a — Human Biology

Q4 a) E.g. to prevent microorganisms getting in from the air.
b) The flame kills any microorganisms already on the loop.
Q5 a) i) 37 °C
ii) It starts to decrease in number. The bacteria could be starting to run out of food / toxins could be building up / they could be overcrowded.
b) 37 °C is human body temperature — he may be interested in how bacteria grow in or on people.
c) At 25 °C, bacteria that are harmful to humans grow more slowly / aren't likely to grow — so they're less likely to get out of control and infect someone.

Page 11 — Fighting Disease — Past and Future

Q1 a) Semmelweis asked all the doctors to wash their hands using antiseptic solution when entering his ward.
This killed bacteria on their hands and stopped them from spreading infections to their next patients.
b) Doctors at this time didn't know about bacteria, so they couldn't see any clear reason to stick to Semmelweis's method.
Q2 a) The number of deaths has fallen dramatically.
b) i) E.g. by overusing antibiotics.
ii) They're working on developing new antibiotics that are effective against resistant strains.
Q3 a) The new strain could be resistant to antibiotics, so current treatments would no longer clear an infection. It could be a new strain that we've not encountered before, so no-one would be immune to it.
b) A big outbreak of disease.
c) Vaccines use dead or inactive microorganisms to stimulate an immune response and prepare the body for future infection. If the microorganism then evolves and changes, the immune system won't recognise it any more and won't be prepared for an infection.

Pages 12-13 — The Nervous System

Q1 E.g. so they can react/respond to the changes and avoid danger.
Q2 Light receptor cells contain a nucleus, cytoplasm and a cell membrane.
Q3 hearing
Q4 a) Chemical receptor. **Tongue** underlined.
b) Chemical receptor. **Nose** underlined.
c) Sound receptor. **Ears** underlined.
d) Pain receptor. **Skin** underlined.
Q5 a) central nervous system
b) brain and spinal cord
c) neurone/nerve cell
Q6 The information from the receptors in the toe can't complete its normal path through the spinal cord to the brain.
Q7 a) i) fingertip
ii) sole of foot
b) The fingertip. This was the most sensitive part of the body to pressure, so it is likely to contain the most receptors.
c) John and Marc might have been applying different pressures, so any differences the pupils noticed might not have been only due to the number of receptors / John and Marc are different, introducing an extra variable so it was not a fair test.
d) Test each pupil a number of times and find the average. Even better, sometimes prod the pupils with one point and at other times with two. Ask them how many points they feel each time.

Pages 14-15 — Synapses and Reflexes

Q1 a) quickly
b) spinal cord
c) protect
d) without
e) receptors
f) neurones
g) chemicals
Q2 a) Eye A has a smaller pupil than Eye B does.
Also accept: Eye A has a bigger iris than Eye B does.
b) Eye A. The pupil has contracted in this diagram to stop too much light entering the eye and damaging it.
c) automatic
d) Automatic responses happen very quickly, so the eye can respond to changes in light intensity as soon as possible. This helps your eyes adjust quickly to dimmer light, and stops them being damaged by sudden bright lights.
Q3 E.g. a reflex reaction happens without you having to take time to think about it.
Q4 a) i) sensory neurone
ii) relay neurone
iii) motor neurone
b) i) electrically
ii) chemically
c) i) effector
ii) It contracts (to pull the finger away).
d) i) synapses
ii) The signal is transferred across the gap by chemicals, which are released when the impulse arrives at one side of the gap. The chemicals diffuse across the gap and trigger a new impulse in the neurone on the other side of the gap.

Page 16 — Hormones

Q1 chemical, glands, blood, target
Q2 a) blood
b) oestrogen
c) FSH
d) glands
e) LH
Q3 Hormones use a chemical signal and nerves use an electrical signal. Responses that are due to hormones happen more slowly and last longer than those that are due to the nervous system. Nerves act on a very precise area, while hormones travel all over the body and can affect more than one area at once.
Q4 a) nervous system
b) hormonal system
c) nervous system
d) nervous system
e) hormonal system

Page 17 — The Menstrual Cycle

Q1 FSH — pituitary gland
oestrogen — ovaries
LH — pituitary gland
Q2 a) 1. Causes an egg to mature in an ovary.
2. Stimulates the ovaries to produce oestrogen.
b) Oestrogen inhibits the production of FSH.
c) It stimulates the release of an egg from the ovary.
Q3 a) & b)

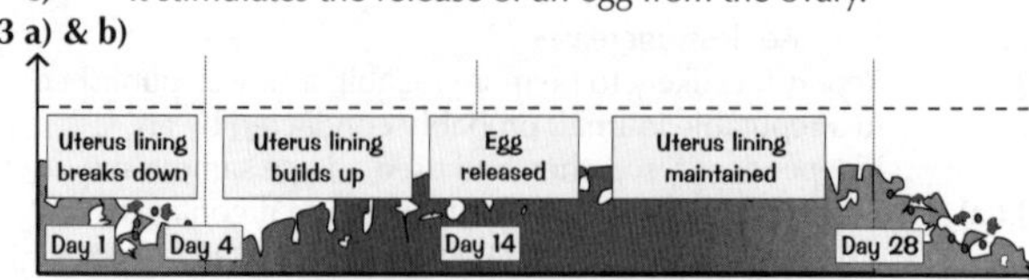

Pages 18-19 — Controlling Fertility

Q1 a) FSH, LH
b) They stimulate egg release in the woman's ovaries.
Q2 a) E.g. it's over 99% effective at preventing pregnancy.
It reduces the risk of getting some types of cancer.
b) Oestrogen is taken every day to give high levels of oestrogen in the blood. This inhibits the release of FSH by the pituitary gland. Eventually egg development in the ovaries stops so that none are released during the menstrual cycle.
c) Because it has fewer side effects.

Biology 1a — Human Biology

Q3 Reducing fertility — any 2 from: Not 100% effective. Causes side effects like nausea, headaches, irregular periods. Doesn't protect against STDs.
Increasing fertility — any 2 from: Doesn't always work, causes side effects like abdominal pain, vomiting and dehydration, can result in multiple births, can be expensive.

Q4 The first version of the pill contained high levels of oestrogen and progesterone, but there were concerns about a link between oestrogen in the pill and side effects like blood clots. The pill now contains a lower dose of oestrogen so has fewer side effects.

Q5 a) FSH and LH are given to the woman to increase the number of eggs that develop. The eggs are collected from her ovaries and fertilised outside the body. They're then allowed to develop into embryos. Once the embryos are tiny balls of cells, one or two are then placed back inside the uterus/womb to improve the chance of pregnancy.

b) **Advantages** — It allows infertile couples to have children. It allows screening of embryos for genetic defects.
Disadvantages — There can be reactions to the hormones, e.g. vomiting, dehydration, abdominal pain. There may be an increased risk of some types of cancer. The process can be expensive, and there's no guarantee that it will work. It may result in multiple births, which can be risky.

Q6 a) 27.5% (accept 27% to 28%)

b) IVF treatment is less likely to be successful as the woman gets older.

c) IVF treatment has a lower success rate in this age group (but is still just as expensive).

Pages 20-21 — Plant Hormones

Q1 a) false
b) false
c) true
d) true
e) false
f) true

Q2 shade, faster, towards, lower, faster, upwards

Q3 a) Seedling A: the foil prevents any light reaching the tip, so the auxin is evenly distributed in the tip and no bending occurs.
Seedling C: the mica strip prevents the auxin from moving to the side that's in the shade, so there is even distribution of auxin and no bending occurs.

b) E.g. Vicky could repeat the experiment to improve the reliability of the results.

Q4 a) It increased crop yield compared to the field without the weedkiller.

b) Plant growth hormones disrupt the normal growth patterns of broad-leaved plants (the weeds) but not crops. (This kills the weeds and allows the crops to grow bigger as there is less competition for nutrients and light.)

Q5 a)

Concentration of auxin (parts per million)	0	0.001	0.01	0.1	1
Length of root at start of investigation (mm)	20	20	20	20	20
Length of root 1 week after investigation started (mm)	26	32	28	23	21
Increase in root length (mm)	6	12	8	3	1

b)

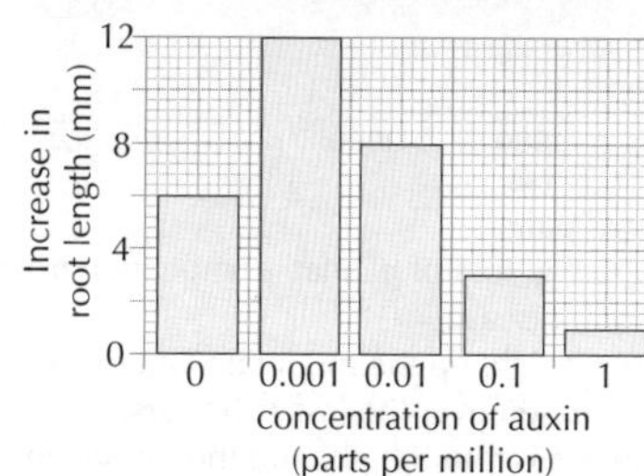

c) 0.001 parts per million

d) High auxin concentration inhibits growth, since the increase in root length is less than when no auxin was added.

e) E.g. He ensured the lengths of all the roots at the beginning were the same.

Pages 22-23 — Homeostasis

Q1 The maintenance of a 'constant internal environment' in the body.

Q2 a) The enzymes controlling all the reactions in the human body don't work as well if the temperature varies too much.

b) The brain.

Q3 a) The person might have done some exercise. / The person might not have eaten for a long time.

b) Eating/drinking foods that are rich in simple carbohydrates, i.e. sugars.

c) To provide the body's cells with a constant supply of energy.

Q4 hot, sweat a lot, less, dark, less, concentrated.

Q5 The following should be ticked:
Ronald loses salt in his sweat.
Ronald's kidneys remove salt from his blood.
Ronald gets rid of salt in his urine.

Q6 a) More water. The exercise will increase his temperature, so he will have to sweat more to cool down.

b) More water. The exercise will make him breathe harder, so more water will be lost via the lungs.

c) Less water. More will be lost as sweat and in the breath, so to balance this the kidneys will give out less water in the urine.

Q7 20th July was hotter so she'd sweat more. More water would be lost through her skin and less would be lost in her urine. Her urine would be more concentrated, so the ion concentration would be higher.

Page 24 — Drugs

Q1 a) A chemical that interferes with reactions in your body.

b) i) Your body can't function normally without the drug, leading to cravings and withdrawal symptoms if the drug is not taken.

ii) E.g. heroin

c) To lower the risk of heart and circulatory disease.

Q2 a) E.g. to increase their heart rate.

b) E.g. the athlete may not be fully informed of the serious risks of stimulants. It makes sporting competitions unfair if an athlete gains an advantage by taking stimulants and not just through hard training.

Q3 Some studies have shown a link, but others have not. Results can often be interpreted in different ways, depending on what the researcher wants to show (and who's funding the study).

Q4 a) As a control group.

b) Statins combined with lifestyle changes helps to reduce cholesterol levels more than just lifestyle changes alone.

Page 25 — Testing Medicinal Drugs

Q1
1. Drug is tested on human cells and tissues
2. Drug is tested on live animals
3. Human volunteers are used to test the drug

Q2 a) To check whether the drugs have any unknown side effects, and to find the optimum dose of each drug.

b) To make sure the drug has no harmful side effects when the body is working normally.

Q3 a) For use as a sleeping pill.

b) It relieved morning sickness, but it also crossed the placenta and stunted the growth of the fetus's limbs.

c) e.g. leprosy

Q4 a) A placebo is a pill that looks like a drug being tested but contains no drug.

b) They use a placebo to make sure it is the actual drug which is causing any effects. Some patients will have beneficial effects just because they *think* they are receiving medicine.

c) A double blind trial is one where neither the scientist doing the test nor the patient knows whether they are getting a drug or a placebo.

Biology 1b — Environment and Evolution

Page 26 — Recreational Drugs

Q1 Liver disease, unconsciousness and addiction should be underlined.

Q2 a) Any two from: e.g. for enjoyment / relaxation/stress relief / inspiration.

b) E.g. they can cause problems with the heart / circulatory system.

Q3 a) Stepping stone — using cannabis makes people want to try harder drugs.

b) Gateway drug — people who use cannabis will have access to drug dealers and so will find it easier to try harder drugs.

c) Genetics — some people are just more likely to use drugs, so people that use cannabis are more likely to use all kinds of drugs.

Q4 a) Because so many more people take them.

b) Any two from: The NHS spends large amounts each year on treating patients with smoking- or drinking-related problems. The cost to businesses of people missing work due to smoking or drinking related problems. The cost of cleaning up the streets, police time, damage to people and property, etc.

Pages 27-29 — Mixed Questions — Biology 1a

Q1 a) The sense organs are the ears, and they contain sound and balance receptors.

b) i) Sensory neurones carry impulses from receptors to the CNS. Motor neurones carry impulses from the CNS to the effectors (muscles and glands).

ii) The nerve signal is transferred by chemicals that diffuse across the synapse and set off a new electrical signal in the next neurone.

c) i) E.g. to increase muscle size

ii) E.g. high blood pressure

Q2 a) 30 days

b) An egg is released / ovulation.

c) Any from: FSH / LH / progesterone.

d) Oestrogen inhibits the production of FSH, which stops egg development and production.

Q3 a) i) Vitamins

ii) Overeating

iii) higher

iv) more

v) energy

b) i) E.g. through the skin as sweat, via the lungs in breath, via the kidneys as urine.

ii) If the air is hotter then more water will be lost through sweat so less urine will be produced.

Q4 a) To see whether the drug works, to find out its toxicity and the best dosage to use.

b) Whether it is published in a reputable journal, whether it was written by a qualified person, whether it was written by someone who may be biased, how large a sample was used.

Q5 true, false, false, true, false

Q6 a) In the blood.

b) slow response, response lasts for a long time

c) i) At the tips of the shoots and roots.

ii) In shoots, auxin makes the cells grow faster. In the roots, auxin slows cell growth.

iii) e.g. weedkiller

Q7 a) The bacteria have been killed by the antibiotic.

b) i) Antibiotic 3.

ii) No, because flu and colds are caused by viruses but antibiotics don't kill viruses.

Biology 1b — Environment and Evolution

Pages 30-31 — Adaptations

Q1 a) The kangaroo rat.

b) The polar bear.

c) The polar bear has a rounded body shape, which means it has a small surface area for its volume.

d) Less heat.

e) It would be bigger than the polar bear's because the desert is very hot, so the kangaroo rat needs to lose more heat than the polar bear, which lives in a cold climate.

Q2 a) In the desert.

b) i) The cactus has spines instead of leaves, because the small surface area gives less of a surface for water to evaporate from. / The spines help to protect the cactus from being eaten by animals.

ii) The cactus has a thick, fleshy stem where it can store water. / The stem can photosynthesise.

iii) The cactus has shallow but very extensive roots, so it can take in as much water as possible when it rains.

Q3 extremophiles, temperature, pressure (or pressure, temperature)

Q4 a) i) white fur

ii) It provides camouflage (white colour makes it hard to spot against a snowy background).

b) It is a warning colour to scare off predators.

c) E.g. thorns on roses / sharp spines on cacti / the shell of a tortoise / poison in bees / poison in poison ivy.

Q5 a) Reading down the table: 1.5 : 1, 1 : 1, 0.75 : 1, 0.6 : 1.

b) The surface area : volume ratio decreases as the size of the cube increases.

c) The small cube, because it has a small volume where it can hold heat but a relatively large surface over which it can lose it.

d) A mouse is small so it would lose heat quickly. Fur provides a layer of insulation to minimise heat loss.

Pages 32-33 — Competition and Environmental Change

Q1 a) Light — Plants
Minerals from the soil — Plants
Space — Plants and Animals
Water — Plants and Animals
Food — Animals
Mates — Animals

b) The two species would have to compete for it.

c) E.g. as a source of food.

Q2 a) Any two from: the temperature of the water increased, the amount of light increased, the amount of nutrients increased, etc.

b) The number of fish in the pond increased rapidly in May (also accept April). Even though the water is warm at this time and there is a lot of light, the number of algae suddenly decreases, so this must be because they are being eaten by fish.

Q3 a)

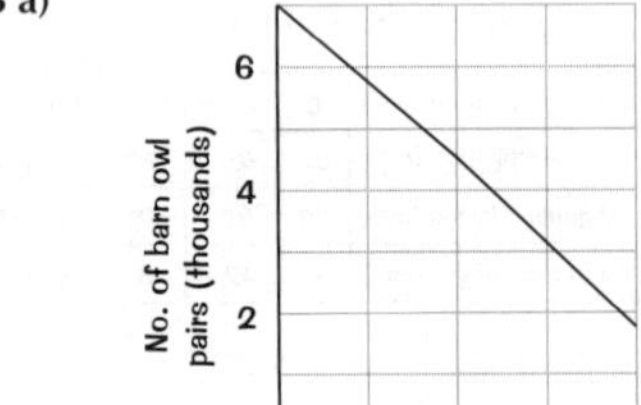

b) 3100 barn owl pairs.

c) Any two from, e.g. loss of habitat, competition from another bird, predation, disease.

Q4 a) The maximum height up the mountain where the snail was found has increased over the last 100 years.

b) The snail species is found higher up the mountain, because it's warmer than it used to be higher up.

c) E.g. average rainfall / air pollution / water pollution

Biology 1b — Environment and Evolution

Page 34 — Measuring Environmental Change

Q1 a) True
b) True
c) False
Q2 a) 1970.
b) About 1 million tonnes.
c) lichen
Q3 a) An indicator species.
b) E.g. collect samples of the same size / in the same way / at the same time of day.
c) Mayfly larvae prefer clean water and sludgeworms prefer water that contains sewage.
d) E.g. Sewage is full of bacteria, which use up a lot of oxygen. Animals like mayfly larvae might not have enough oxygen to survive.

Page 35 — Pyramids of Biomass

Q1 a) algae
b) winkle
c) algae/producers
Q2 a) C
b) The total mass of the organisms decreases at each trophic level as shown by this pyramid.
c) Their energy initially comes from the Sun.
Q3 a) The levels of DDT increase dramatically as you go up the trophic levels.
b) i) 13.8 ÷ 0.04 = **345**
ii) 2.8 ÷ 0.04 = **70**
c) DDT is stored in the tissues of animals and a pyramid of biomass represents the mass of the living tissues.

Pages 36-37 — Energy Transfer and Decay

Q1 a) true
b) true
c) true
d) true
e) false
f) false
Q2 Any three from:
Decomposers — Adding more decomposers will speed up decay.
Shredded waste — Shredding the waste gives more surface area for the microorganisms to work on.
Base in contact with soil — More microorganisms will have access to the contents of the compost bin.
Mesh sides — These allow contact with the air, so plenty of oxygen is available to help the microorganisms work faster.
Open top — This allows contact with the air, so plenty of oxygen is available to help the microorganisms work faster.
Q3 a) energy
b) plants, photosynthesis
c) eat
d) respiration
e) lost, movement
f) inedible, hair
Q4 1. Plants take up minerals from the soil.
2. Plants use minerals and the products of photosynthesis to make complex nutrients.
3. Nutrients in plants are passed to animals through feeding and used in respiration to provide energy.
4. Energy released in respiration is lost by decay, heat and movement and the production of waste.
5. Waste and dead tissues are decayed by microorganisms.
6. Materials are recycled and returned to the soil by decay.
Q5 a) i) E.g. carbon, nitrogen, oxygen, hydrogen
ii) From the soil, air, water or eating other plants and animals.
b) When animals die or produce waste, microorganisms cause these materials to decay. The process of decay releases the elements back to the soil, air or water again for plants to use. The plants are then eaten by animals.
Q6 a) not stable
b) stable
c) not stable
d) stable
Q7 a) (2070 ÷ 103 500) × 100 = 2%
b) 2070 ÷ 10 = 207
207 – (90 + 100) = 17 kJ
c) E.g. heat loss / movement / excretion
d) So much energy is lost at each stage of a food chain that there's not enough left to support more organisms after about five stages.

Page 38 — The Carbon Cycle

Q1 carbon dioxide, photosynthesis, respiration, microorganisms, eating, carbohydrates, waste, detritus
Q2 Plants use — carbon dioxide to build complex molecules.
Microorganisms release — carbon dioxide by decaying waste and dead tissue.
Animals and plants release — carbon dioxide through respiration.
Animals take in — carbon through feeding.
Plants take in — carbon by photosynthesis.
Q3 a) fossil fuel (accept coal or oil)
b) combustion / burning

Pages 39-40 — Variation

Q1 have differences, genes, gametes, Identical twins, hair style, environment, variation
Q2 a) No. Identical twins have exactly the same genes. Features like hair colour are controlled by genes, so you would expect the girls to have the same hair colour.
b) The difference in weight must be due to environment (e.g. eating more or exercising less), because the twins have exactly the same genes.
c) I don't think that birthmarks are caused by genes. Identical twins have exactly the same genes, so if Stephanie had a birthmark then Helen should too if it was genetic.
Q3 a) Sexual reproduction gives new combinations of genes, so the foal might not be genetically suited to racing. / Organisms are affected by their environment as well as their genes.
b) Genes.
Q4 a) The lighter moth was better camouflaged against the bark of the trees, so it was less likely to be spotted and eaten by birds.
b) As industry increased, the trees became darkened with soot. Now the dark moths were better camouflaged, so they increased in number.
c) Genes.
Q5 a) These plants have very different characteristics because they are different species and so have different genes.
b) Organisms that reproduce by sexual reproduction receive different combinations of genes, so each organism has its own unique characteristics.
c) The strawberry plants may have been grown in different environments (also accept: The plants may not have had the same parent.)

Page 41 — Genes, Chromosomes and DNA

Q1 nucleus, chromosomes, DNA, genes
Q2 gene, chromosome, nucleus, cell.
Q3 'Alleles' are different forms of the same gene.
Q4 There are two chromosome 7s in a human nucleus, one from each parent.
Q5 a) 2
b) 2
c) 1

Biology 1b — Environment and Evolution

Page 42 — Reproduction

Q1 a) two
b) gametes
c) identical
d) half as many
e) Sexual
Q2 a) clones
b) sperm
c) fertilisation
Q3 a) The new skin cells came from the existing skin cells around the cut dividing to give new cells.
b) Asexual reproduction produces cells with identical genes to the parent cells.
c) It took time for the cells to divide enough times to cover the cut completely.
Q4 Sexual reproduction involves the production of gametes by each parent. Each gamete has half the normal number of chromosomes. The gametes fuse together and a baby with a full set of chromosomes is produced.

Pages 43-44 — Cloning

Q1 Parent plant → Cuttings are taken, each with a new bud on → The cuttings are kept in moist conditions until they are ready to plant → Cloned plant
Q2 a) A few plant cells are put into a growth medium with hormones and they grow into new plants / clones of the parent plant.
b) Any two from: e.g. new plants can be made very quickly. / They can be made in very little space. / They can be grown at different times of the year.
Q3 removing and discarding a nucleus = **A**
implantation in a surrogate mother = **D**
useful nucleus extracted = **B**
formation of a diploid cell = **C**
Q4 a) False
b) False
c) True
d) False
e) True
Q5 genetically, nucleus, egg, donor, electric shock, dividing, genetically, donor
Q6 E.g. cloning quickly gets you lots of ideal offspring. But you also get a population with a reduced gene pool — so if a new disease appears, they could all be wiped out. The study of animal clones could improve our understanding of the development of the embryo / of ageing and age-related disorders. Cloning could also be used to help preserve endangered species. However, it's possible that cloned animals might not be as healthy as normal ones. Some people worry that humans might be cloned in the future and any success may follow many unsuccessful attempts, e.g. children born severely disabled.

Pages 45-46 — Genetic Engineering

Q1 a) The purpose of the trial was to see what effect growing herbicide-tolerant GM crops would have on wildlife.
b) i) So that both types of crop experienced the same conditions — otherwise it wouldn't have been a fair test.
ii) Both halves of the fields were ploughed in the same way, and given the same amount of fertiliser etc. This makes it a fair test.
iii) The herbicide was applied differently, because tolerating more herbicide is the advantage that herbicide-resistant crops have and if they were widely grown in the UK, more herbicide would be used.
c) i) Farmers are able to use more herbicide on crops that are herbicide-resistant, so more weeds are killed. If they use too much on normal plants, they risk damaging the crop as well as the weeds.
ii) farmers: Farmers would have bigger crop yields, because there would be fewer weeds to compete with their crops. This would make them more money.
shopper buying these products: If farmers were producing bigger yields, they could afford to sell their products more cheaply. This would save shoppers money. / The products produced would be of a better quality.
d) The result was surprising because there were more weeds with the GM crop even though more herbicide was used.
e) i) Yes they do, because most of the GM crops had less wildlife living amongst the plants.
ii) E.g. people are worried that they may not be safe to eat. There are also concerns that transplanted genes may get out into the natural environment.
iii) E.g. the herbicide-resistance gene may have been picked up by the weeds. / The herbicide may not have been applied properly on the GM plants. / Conditions may have been better for the weeds in those parts of the fields for another reason, e.g. amount of light.

Pages 47-48 — Evolution

Q1

	Plant	Animal
Travels to new places		X
Makes its own food	X	
Is fixed to the ground	X	
May be single celled		

Q2 a) Rays and Sharks
b) E.g. they could be in competition.
Q3 There is variation within species caused by differences in their genes.
The best adapted animals and plants are most likely to survive.
Some characteristics are passed on through reproduction from parent to offspring.
Q4 1. Ancestors to the buff tip moth showed variation in their appearance. Some had genes that made them look a bit like a stick.
2. Short-sighted birds in poor light didn't spot the stick-like moths.
3. So the stick-like moths were more likely to survive and reproduce.
4. Genes that made the moths look like sticks were more likely to be passed on to the next generation.
Q5 a) E.g. longer legs would help when running away from predators. B has a hoof rather than toes. This makes it more stable when running. The environment may have changed from rocky slopes or swamps (where toes would help with balance) to flat plains (where balance is less important).
b)

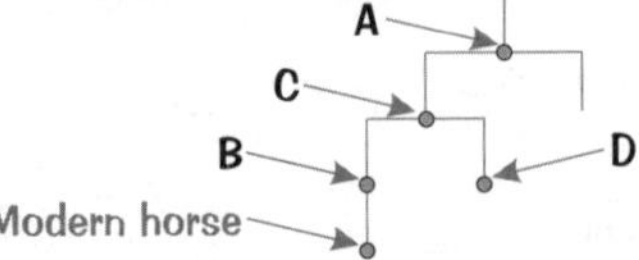

Q6 A small number of the original bacteria were naturally resistant to the antibiotic. These bacteria survived the antibiotic and reproduced to form the second plaque.
All the bacteria in the second plaque inherited the antibiotic resistance.

Page 49 — More About Evolution

Q1 A, E
Q2 Lamarck, more developed, longer, the next generation
Q3 People with dyed blue hair do not have children with blue hair.
Sheep whose tails are cut short give birth to lambs with full-length tails.
Q4 Any two from, e.g. because they have different beliefs / because they have been influenced by different people / because they think differently.

Biology 2a — Cells, Organs and Populations

Pages 50-52 — Mixed Questions — Biology 1b

Q1 a) i) It increased.
ii) It stayed constant.
b) The goat.
c) Because they lose too much water, and water is scarce in the desert.
d) natural selection

Q2 a) Donkeys have 62 chromosomes and horses have 64 chromosomes, so mules will have 63 chromosomes.
b) Ligers have chromosomes that can all pair up, because lions and tigers have the same number of chromosomes. Mules have one chromosome that can't pair up, so their chromosome pairs can't split up to make normal gametes.

Q3 a) Egg A. The parents of egg A provided the genetic material that was inserted into egg B, so the toad inherited its features from these parents.
b) Dolly was a clone because she was produced using genetic material from a single sheep. The fertilised cell used in the toad experiment contained a mixture of genes from two parents, so was not a clone.
c) E.g. space and food
d) Species that are sensitive to slight changes in their environment (so can be used to indicate environmental conditions).

Q4 a) To check that the gene for growth hormone had been inserted successfully. The piece of DNA that was inserted contained both these genes, so if the bacteria were resistant to the penicillin they would also be able to produce growth hormone.
b) E.g. bacteria reproduce quickly.
c) asexual

Q5 a) i) 43 700 – 7500 = **36 200 kJ**
ii) 7500 ÷ 43 700 × 100 = **17%**
b) E.g. in maintaining a constant body temperature / in waste materials.
c) A — respiration
B — feeding / ingestion / digestion
C — death and waste
D — CO_2 release from decay / respiration by decomposers
E — photosynthesis
F — respiration
d) The high temperature and good availability of oxygen will increase the rate of decomposition, as microorganisms work well in these conditions.

Biology 2a — Cells, Organs and Populations

Page 53 — Cells

Q1 a) Plant, animal
b) cell wall
c) Both plant and animal cells, proteins
d) membrane

Q2 a) The **nucleus** contains genetic material / chromosomes / genes / DNA. Its function is controlling the cell's activities.
b) **Chloroplasts** contain chlorophyll. Their function is to make food by photosynthesis.
c) The **cell wall** is made of cellulose. Its function is to support the cell and strengthen it.

Q3 a) animal
b) E.g.

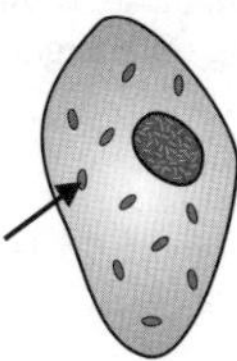

c) Respiration happens inside mitochondria, which provides energy for life processes.

Q4 a) cell wall
b) cell membrane
c) cytoplasm
d) Because the genetic material is floating in the cytoplasm and not in a nucleus.

Pages 54-55 — Diffusion

Q1 random, higher, lower, net, bigger, gases

Q2 a)

(The dye particles will have spread out evenly.)
b) The rate of diffusion would **speed up**.
c) The dye particles will move from an area of higher concentration (the drop of dye) to an area of lower concentration (the water).

Q3 a) Switching a fan on will spread the curry particles more quickly through the house.
b) The curry will smell stronger. Adding more curry powder increases the concentration of the curry particles and increases the rate of diffusion of the curry particles to the air.

Q4 a) False
b) False
c) True
d) True
e) False

Q5 a) B
b) There is a greater concentration difference between the two sides of the membrane in model B so the molecules will diffuse faster.

Q6 a) glucose
b) Starch molecules are too large to fit through the pores in the membrane, but the small glucose molecules would diffuse through to the area of lower glucose concentration outside the bag.

Page 56 — Specialised Cells

Q1 a) red blood cells
b) sperm cell
c) guard cells
d) egg cell / ovum

Q2 Lots of chloroplasts... for photosynthesis.
Tall shape... gives a large surface area for absorbing CO_2.
Thin shape... means you can pack more cells in at the top of the leaf.

Q3 stomata, turgid, photosynthesis, flaccid, night.

Q4 a) Concave discs / biconcave discs
b) It gives them a large surface area for absorbing oxygen.
c) To leave even more room for haemoglobin / carrying oxygen.

Q5 a) Sperm
b) Sperm
c) Egg
d) Sperm
e) Sperm

Pages 57-58 — Cell Organisation

Q1

Cell	Tissue	Organ	Organ System	Organism
sperm egg (human) white blood cell	blood muscle	stomach eye heart liver small intestine	digestive system reproductive system excretory system	snail cat dog

Biology 2a — Cells, Organs and Populations

Q2 a) True
b) False
c) True
d) True
e) True
f) False
g) True
Q3 epithelial cells, epithelial tissue, stomach, digestive system, human
Q4 a) materials, nutrients, bile, organs, liver, tissues, muscular tissue, churn
b) It makes digestive juices that digest food.
c) E.g. pancreas, salivary glands.
Q5 a) To exchange and transport materials.
b) The process by which cells become specialised for a particular job.
Q6 a) A group of similar cells that work together to carry out a particular function.
b) A group of different tissues that work together to perform a certain function.
c) A group of organs working together to perform a particular function.

Pages 59-60 — Plant Structure and Photosynthesis

Q1 water + carbon dioxide → glucose + oxygen
Q2 a) E.g. stems, roots, leaves
b) Mesophyll tissue — it's where most of the photosynthesis in a plant occurs.
Epidermal tissue — it covers the whole plant.
Xylem and phloem — it transports water, mineral ions and sucrose around the plant.
Q3 a) 00.00 (midnight)
b) There's no light at night so photosynthesis won't occur.
c) Plants use the food / glucose (from photosynthesis) they have stored during the day.
d)

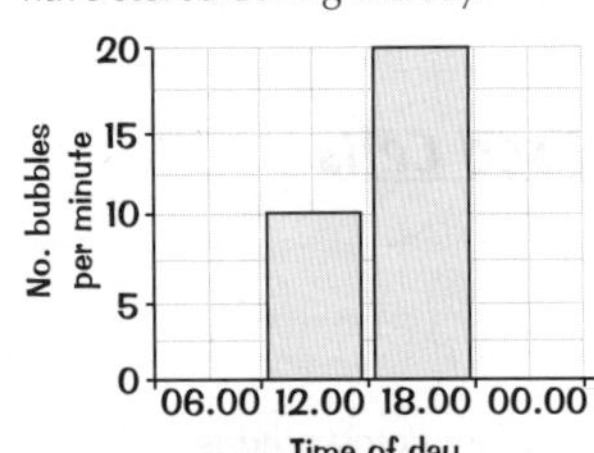

Q4 a) i) Gas A = carbon dioxide
Gas B = oxygen
ii) As it gets lighter, the level of oxygen should increase as the plant will photosynthesise more and produce more oxygen. Carbon dioxide levels should decrease as light intensity increases, because the plant uses up carbon dioxide in photosynthesis.
b) i) As light intensity increases, the amount of carbon dioxide decreases.
ii) As light intensity increases, the amount of oxygen increases.
Q5 a) Plant B
b) The plant in the dark can't photosynthesise and so only has stored starch. The plant in sunlight is able to carry out photosynthesis and produce more glucose, which is then changed to more starch and stored in the leaves.
c) In the chloroplasts.

Pages 61-63 — The Rate of Photosynthesis

Q1 a) E.g. light intensity, CO_2 concentration, temperature
b) A factor that stops photosynthesis from happening any faster.
c) E.g. time of day (such as night time) / position of plant (such as in the shade).
Q2 a) It increases the rate of photosynthesis up to a certain point.
b) The rate of photosynthesis does not continue to increase because temperature or levels of carbon dioxide act as limiting factors.
Q3 a) blue light (approx. 440 nm), red light (approx. 660 nm)
b) You could use blue or red light bulbs to increase the rate of photosynthesis, and therefore the growth rate.
Q4 So that his plants grow well but so that he's not giving them more CO_2 than they need, as this would be wasting money.
Q5 a) the rate of photosynthesis
b)

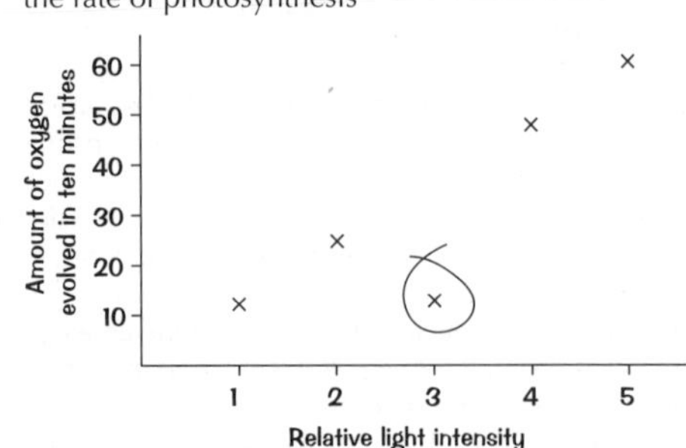

c) i) See circled point on graph.
ii) E.g. she might have collected the gas for less time than 10 minutes. / She might have accidentally used a lower light intensity. / She might have misread the syringe.
d) The rate of photosynthesis increased as light intensity increased.
e) The relationship would continue up to a point, and then the graph would level off. At this point, either the temperature or carbon dioxide level would be acting as a limiting factor.
Q6 a) amount of light and temperature
b) The faster the rate of photosynthesis, the faster the growth rate of the grass.
Q7 a) Any three from, e.g: it traps heat to make sure temperature does not become a limiting factor. / Artificial light can be used to enable photosynthesis to occur at all times. / Carbon dioxide can be maintained at a high level. / Plants can be kept free from pests. / Fertilisers can be added to provide all the necessary minerals for healthy plant growth.
b) i) a heater / artificial light / insulation
ii) ventilation or shades
iii) artificial lights
iv) To produce carbon dioxide and so increase carbon dioxide levels in the greenhouse, thus increasing the rate of photosynthesis.
Q8 a)

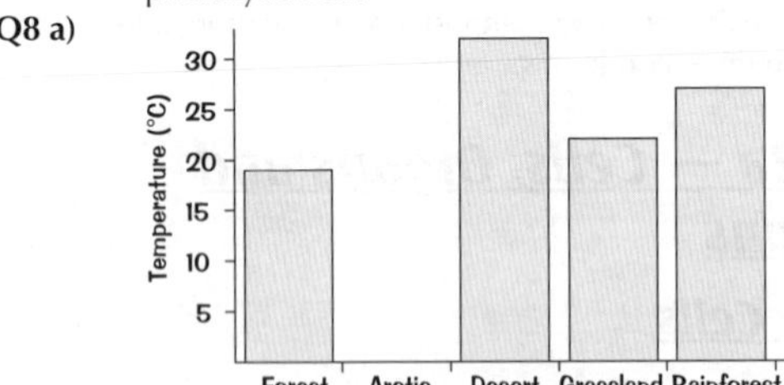

b) Arctic
c) The temperatures are extremely low there, so the rate of photosynthesis will be slower because the enzymes needed for photosynthesis will be working very slowly.
d) Despite the high temperatures, few plants grow in the desert because there is not enough water for them to survive.

Page 64 — How Plants Use Glucose

Q1 leaves, energy, convert, cells, cellulose, walls, lipids, margarine, cooking oil / cooking oil, margarine
Q2 a) nitrate ions
b) dhal — approx. 67%
steak — approx. 64%
c) Dhal, as it contains significantly more B vitamins, calcium and iron, than steak.
d) from plants
Q3 a) They change starch to glucose and use it for respiration to release energy for growth.
b) They use their leaves to make glucose by photosynthesis.

Biology 2b — Enzymes and Genetics

c) They store starch, which is insoluble, so they don't draw in loads of water and swell up as they would if they stored glucose.

Page 65 — Distribution of Organisms

Q1 a) True
b) False
c) True
Q2 Any three from, e.g: temperature / availability of water / availability of oxygen and carbon dioxide / availability of nutrients / amount of light.
Q3 a) A square frame enclosing a known area.
b) E.g. he could divide the field into a grid and use a random number generator to pick coordinates.
c) i) $(3 + 1 + 2 + 1 + 4 + 3 + 0 + 2) \div 8 = 2$ daisies per quadrat
ii) 0,1,1,2,2,3,3,4 so middle value (median) is 2
d) 5 600 x 2 = 11 200 daisies

Page 66 — More on the Distribution of Organisms

Q1 a) i) E.g.

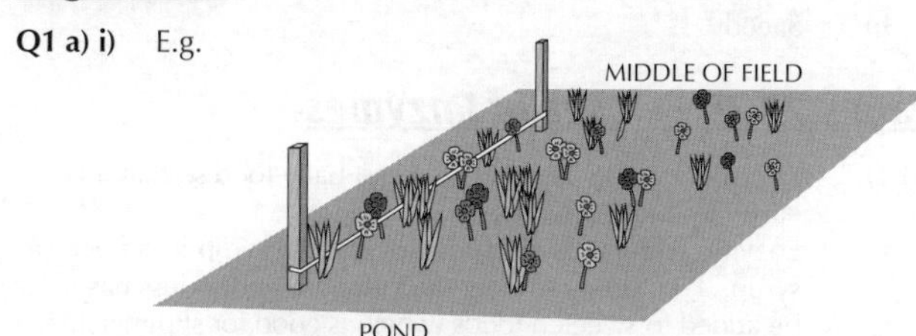

ii) E.g. she could collect data along the line by counting all the buttercups that touch it.
b) E.g. by having a larger sample size.
c) i) The number of buttercups decreases as you go further away from the pond.
ii) E.g. there is more water in the soil nearest to the pond, so more buttercups will grow there.
Q2 Bill's data isn't valid as it doesn't answer his question. The distribution of the dandelions could also be affected by the different soil moisture levels caused by the stream near the wood — he hasn't controlled all the variables.

Pages 67-69 — Mixed Questions — Biology 2a

Q1 Tissue — A group of similar cells that work together to carry out a certain function.
Diffusion — The spreading out of particles from an area of high concentration to an area of low concentration.
Habitat — The place where an organism lives.
Mode — The most common value in a set of data.
Photosynthesis — The process that produces 'food' (glucose) in plants and algae.
Limiting factor — Something that stops photosynthesis from happening any faster.
Differentiation — The process by which cells become specialised for a particular job.
Q2 a) chloroplasts, vacuole, cell wall
b) i)

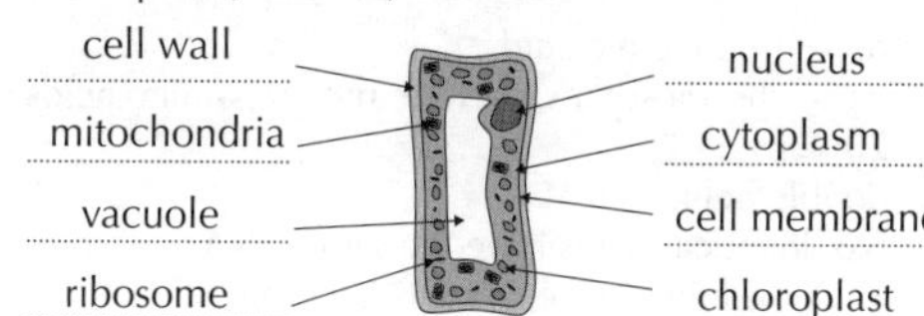

ii) chloroplasts / tall shape
Chloroplasts: contain chlorophyll for photosynthesis.
Tall shape: allows more palisade cells to be packed at the top of the leaf, and increases the surface area down the side of the cells for absorption of carbon dioxide / gaseous exchange.
Q3 a) chlorophyll
b) carbon dioxide, water
c) i) starch
ii) E.g. roots / stems / leaves
d) For respiration, for making proteins, for making cell walls.
Q4 a) i) mitochondria
ii) cytoplasm
b) It contracts (shortens) to move whatever it's attached to.
c) i) To digest food. / To absorb soluble food molecules.
ii) To absorb water from undigested food.
d) i) and ii)

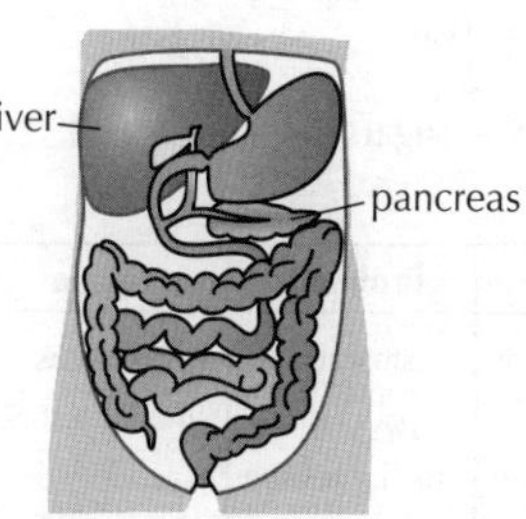

Q5 a) diffusion
b) Z particles are larger than X and Y particles.
c) Protein solution, because protein molecules are bigger than amino acid or glucose molecules.
Q6 a) A quadrat.
b) Total area = 250 m x 180 m = 45 000 m^2
Total area x number of plants = population
45 000 m^2 x 11 = **495 000**, so there's likely to be approximately 500 000 clover plants.
c) i) $(11 + 9 + 8 + 9 + 7) \div 5 = 8.8$ plants
ii) (It is the same field, so use 45 000 m^2 again.)
45 000 m^2 x 8.8 = 396 000 clover plants (≈ 400 000).
d) Lisa's result is likely to be more accurate as she has used a larger sample size.

Biology 2b — Enzymes and Genetics

Pages 70-71 — Enzymes

Q1 a) Enzymes are biological catalysts.
b)

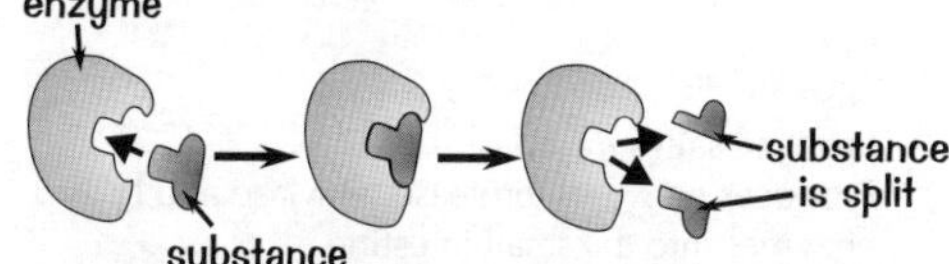

Q2 catalyst, increases, proteins, amino acids, structural, hormones
Q3 a) 33 °C (accept 32 °C – 34 °C)
b) They are denatured.
Q4 a)

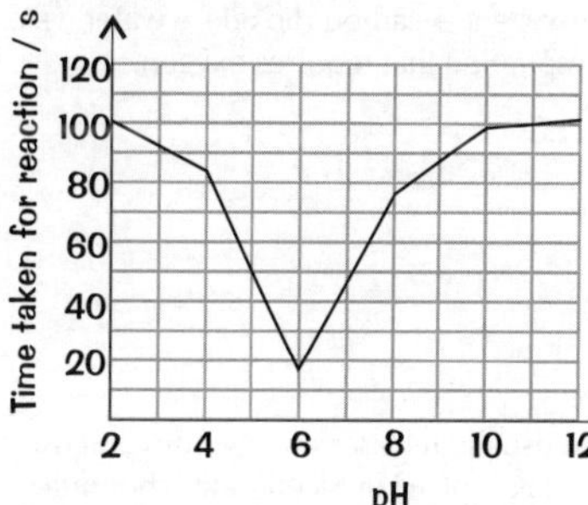

b) About pH 6.
c) At very high and very low pH levels the bonds in the enzymes are broken / the enzyme is denatured, meaning that it can't speed up the reaction.
d) No. This enzyme works very slowly at pH 2.
e) Any two from: the temperature should be the same at each pH / the same volume of the reactant and enzyme should be used for each pH / the same method of determining when the reaction is complete should be used for each pH / he should measure and time everything as accurately as possible using appropriate equipment.

Biology 2b — Enzymes and Genetics

Page 72 — Enzymes and Digestion

Q1 a) **protease**
↓
protein → **amino acids**

b) lipase
↓
fat → **glycerol** + **fatty acids**

c) **amylase**
↓
carbohydrate → **sugars**
e.g. starch

Q2

Amylase	Protease	Lipase	Bile
salivary glands pancreas small intestine	stomach pancreas small intestine	pancreas small intestine	liver

Q3 a) gall bladder, small intestine, neutralises, enzymes, fat.

b) Emulsification breaks fat into smaller droplets which gives a larger surface area for lipase to work on, speeding up digestion.

Page 73 — More on Enzymes and Digestion

Q1

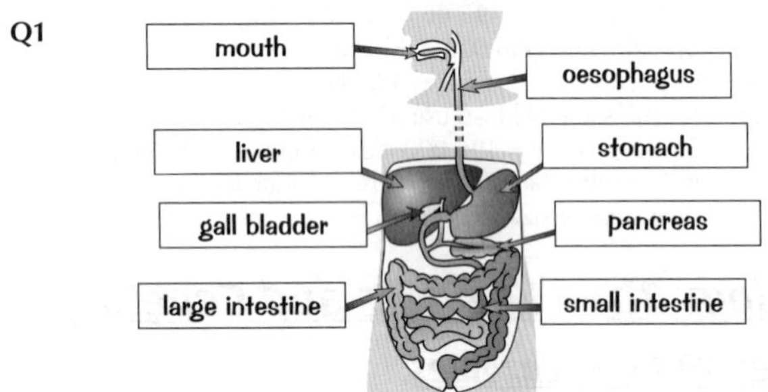

Q2 a) false
b) true
c) true
d) false

Q3 a) Produce saliva / amylase
b) Produces enzymes (protease, amylase and lipase) / releases enzymes into the small intestine.
c) Produces bile which emulsifies fats and neutralises stomach acid.

Page 74 — Enzymes and Respiration

Q1 a) glucose + oxygen → carbon dioxide + water (+ energy)
b) It means respiration that requires oxygen.

Q2 a) i) true
ii) false
iii) true
iv) false
v) true
vi) false
vii) true
viii) true

b) ii) Respiration usually releases energy from glucose.
iv) Respiration takes place in a cell's mitochondria.
vi) Breathing and respiration are completely separate processes.

Q3 E.g. building larger molecules from smaller ones, to allow muscles to contract (in animals), to maintain a certain body temperature (in mammals and birds) and to build sugars, nitrates and other nutrients into amino acids, which are then built up into proteins (in plants).

Pages 75-76 — Exercise

Q1 a) energy, contracting
b) glucose, oxygen
c) rapidly, glycogen
d) anaerobic
e) incomplete

Q2 a) Any two from: e.g. his breathing rate increases / he breathes more deeply / his heart rate increases.
b) i) muscle fatigue
ii) lactic acid
iii) anaerobic respiration
c) While John was respiring anaerobically he created an oxygen debt. When he stops exercising this must be repaid. To do this he breathes deeply to get the necessary oxygen into the muscles to oxidise the lactic acid.

Q3 a) Anaerobic: glucose → lactic acid (+ energy)
b) less

Q4 a) 45 – 15 = **30** breaths per minute
b) The breathing rate increases to provide more oxygen for increased respiration in the muscles and to remove the extra carbon dioxide produced.
c) 3.5 minutes

Q5 a) Any two from, e.g: measuring their pulse rates by averaging over the same time period. / They should run the same distance. / They should run at the same speed.
b) Saeed

Pages 77-78 — Uses of Enzymes

Q1 a) Enzymes can be used to pre-digest baby food so that it is easier for babies to digest.
b) Enzymes can be used to convert glucose syrup into fructose syrup. Fructose is sweeter than glucose and so less has to be added to sweeten foods (which is good for slimmers).

Q2 a) Lipaclean would be best because it contains lipase enzymes and they digest fat.
b) Because they are allergic to them.

Q3 a) carbohydrates
b) isn't, is
c) carbohydrases

Q4 a) E.g. to speed up reactions.
b) Any two from: temperature, pH and lack of contamination.
c) i) Any two from: e.g you can use lower temperatures and pressures, which means a lower cost as it saves energy / enzymes are specific, so they only catalyse the reaction you want them to / they work for a long time so you can continually use them / they are biodegradable (so they cause less pollution).
ii) E.g. they can be denatured by a small change in temperature / they can be denatured by small changes in pH / they are susceptible to poisons / they can cause allergies / they can be expensive to produce.

Q5 a) E.g. use the same amount of each washing powder / use the same type of food stains / use clothes made of the same type of fabric.
b) i) Powder A
ii) Powder A. Biological detergents contain enzymes, so at low temperatures they work more effectively than other detergents.

Pages 79-80 — DNA

Q1 a) deoxyribonucleic acid
b) cells, chromosomes, section, protein, amino acids
c) 20
d) double helix
e) No, identical twins have the same DNA.

Q2 1. Collect the sample for DNA testing.
2. Cut the DNA into small sections.
3. Separate the sections of DNA.
4. Compare the unique patterns of DNA.

Q3 a) E.g. DNA from a crime scene could be checked against everyone in the country.
b) E.g. it might be an invasion of privacy. / False positives could occur if there was a mistake in the analysis.

Biology 2b — Enzymes and Genetics

Q4

	Foal	Mother	Father
DNA sample	Sample 1	Sample 2	**Sample 4**

Q5 a) The victim and suspect A — they share a significant amount of their DNA.
b) Suspect B
c) Suspect B's DNA matches the DNA found at the crime scene.
d) No. If suspect B's blood was found on the victim's shirt, it doesn't mean that he/she committed the murder. Their blood could have got onto the shirt on a different occasion.

Page 81 — Cell Division — Mitosis

Q1 a) true
b) false (there are 23 pairs of chromosomes)
c) false (they're found in the nucleus)
d) true
e) true
f) true
g) true
Q2 a) Cells that are not dividing contain long strings of DNA.
b) Before a cell divides, it copies (duplicates) its DNA and forms X-shaped chromosomes.
c) The chromosomes line up across the centre of the cell, and then the arms of each chromosome are pulled to opposite ends of the cell.
d) A membrane forms in each half of the cell to form the nuclei.
e) The cytoplasm divides, making two new genetically identical cells.
Q3 reproduce, strawberry, runners, asexual, genes, variation.

Pages 82-83 — Cell Division — Meiosis

Q1 a) true
b) true
c) true
d) true
e) false
Q2 a) Before the cell starts to divide it duplicates its DNA to produce an exact copy.
b) For the first meiotic division the chromosomes line up in their pairs across the centre of the cell.
c) The pairs are pulled apart. Each new cell has only one copy of each chromosome, some from the mother and some from the father.
d) The chromosomes line up across the centre of the nucleus ready for the second division, and the left and right arms are pulled apart.
e) There are now 4 gametes, each containing half the original number of chromosomes.
Q3 a) two
b) 46, 23
c) different
d) half as many
Q4 a)

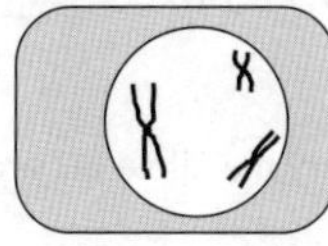

b)

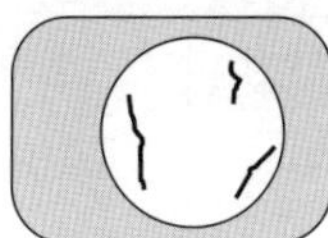

Q5 a) Sex cells that only have one copy of each chromosome.
b) Gametes have half the usual number of chromosomes so that when two gametes join together during fertilisation the resulting fertilised egg will have the full number of chromosomes.
c) When two gametes fuse, the new individual will have a mixture of two sets of chromosomes — some from its mother and some from its father.
d) mitosis

Page 84 — Stem Cells

Q1 specialised, animal, plant, stem cells
Q2 Embryonic stem cells can differentiate into any type of body cell. Adult stem cells are less versatile — they can only turn into certain types of cell.
Q3 E.g. people with some blood diseases (e.g. sickle cell anaemia) can be treated by bone marrow transplants. Bone marrow contains stem cells that can turn into new blood cells to replace the faulty old ones.
Q4 diabetes — insulin-producing cells
paralysis — nerve cells
heart disease — heart muscle cells
Q5 a) E.g. stem cell research may lead to cures for a wide variety of diseases.
b) E.g. embryos shouldn't be used for experiments as each one is a potential human life.

Page 85 — X and Y Chromosomes

Q1 a) true
b) false
c) true
d) false
Q2 a)

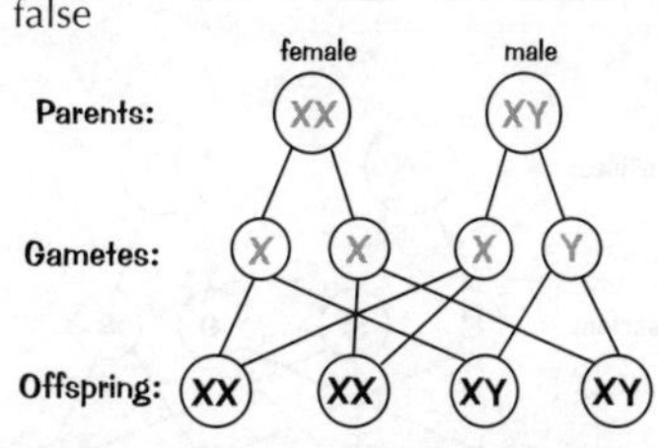

b) The probability is 50% (0.5, 1 in 2, ½).
Q3 a) ZW
b)

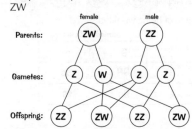

female male
Parents: ZW ZZ
Gametes: Z W Z Z
Offspring: ZZ ZW ZZ ZW

Page 86 — The Work of Mendel

Q1 monk, characteristics, generation, 1866, genetics.
Q2 a) E.g. hereditary units determine the characteristics of an organism. They're passed from parents to offspring. The modern word for them is genes.
b) The dominant hereditary unit is expressed.
Q3 a)

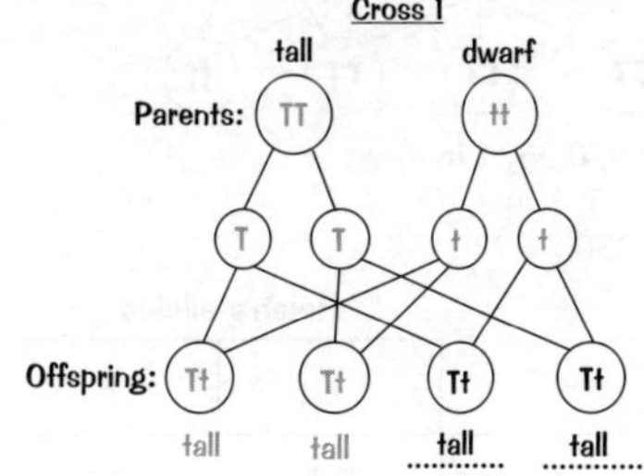

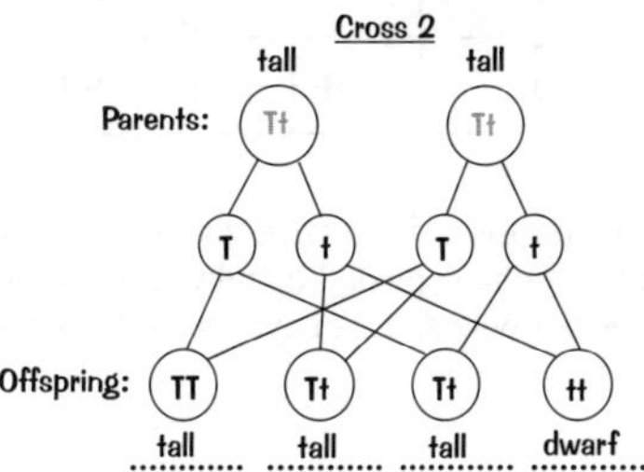

b) 75% (0.75, 3 in 4, ¾)

Biology 2b — Enzymes and Genetics

Pages 87-88 — Genetic Diagrams

Q1 dominant — shown in organisms heterozygous for that trait
genotype — the alleles that an individual contains
heterozygous — having two different alleles for a gene
homozygous — having two identical alleles for a gene
phenotype — the actual characteristics of an individual
recessive — not shown in organisms heterozygous for that trait

Q2 a) Wilma will have brown hair.
b) Wilma has two different alleles for this gene so she is heterozygous for the characteristic.

Q3 a) i) red eyes
ii) white eyes
iii) red eyes
iv) white eyes
b) i)

		parent's alleles	
		R	r
parent's alleles	R	RR	Rr
	r	Rr	rr

ii) 1/4 or 25%
iii) 12

Q4 a)

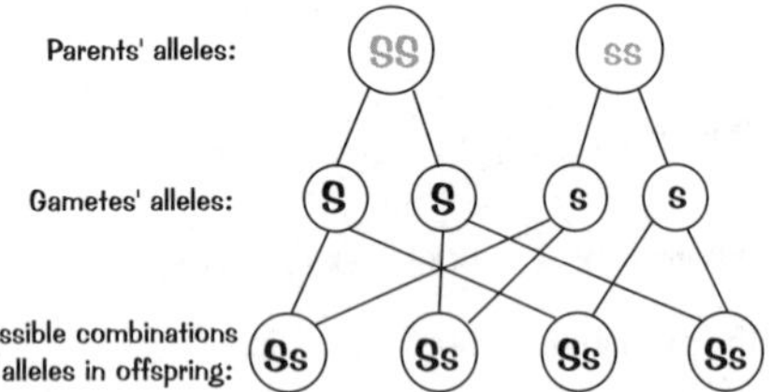

b) 0% chance of being wrinkled
c)

		parent's alleles	
		S	s
parent's alleles	S	SS	Ss
	s	Ss	ss

d) True

Pages 89-90 — Genetic Disorders

Q1 a)

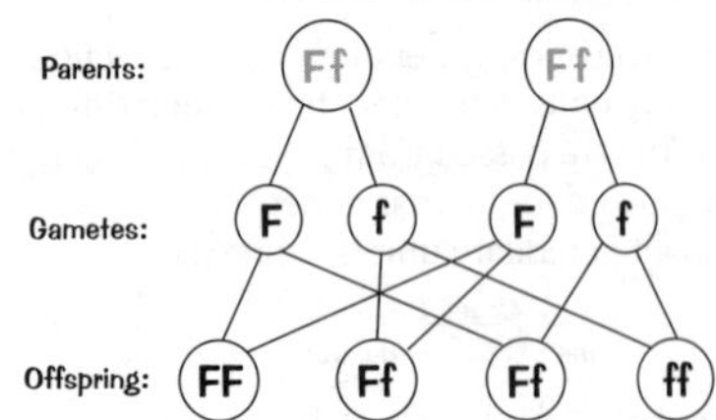

b) i) 25% (quarter, 0.25, 1 in 4, ¼)
ii) 50% (half, 0.5, 1 in 2, ½)
c) 600 000 ÷ 2500 = 240

Q2 a) i)

		Helen's alleles	
		F	F
John's alleles	F	F F	F F
	f	F f	F f

ii) 0
b) No — cystic fibrosis is a recessive disease, so to suffer from it you must inherit a copy of the faulty allele from both parents. (Mark's wife doesn't have the faulty allele.)

Q3 a) i)

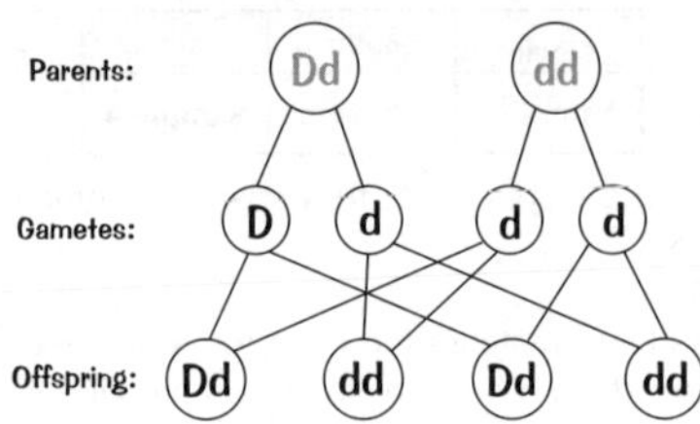

ii) 50% (or 0.5 or ½)
b) A sufferer. Since polydactyly is a dominant disorder, you only need one copy of the defective allele to have it.
c) 100% (or 1)

Q4 a) Possible answers include:
- Embryonic screening implies that genetic disorders are 'undesirable' and may increase prejudice against people with these diseases.
- The rejected embryos are destroyed. Each one could be a human life.
- There's a risk that embryonic screening could be taken too far, e.g. parents might want to choose embryos who fulfil their vision of the ideal child.

b) Possible answers include:
- If embryonic screening means healthy children are born, then this stops the suffering associated with many genetic disorders.
- During IVF, most of the embryos are destroyed anyway — screening just allows the selected one to be healthy.

Pages 91-92 — More Genetic Diagrams

Q1 a)

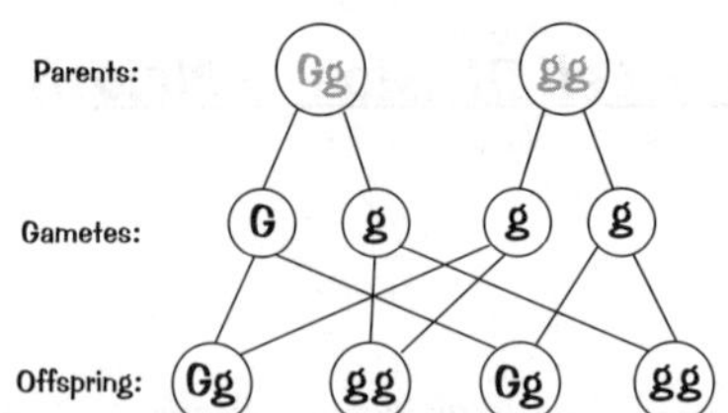

b) 1 : 1 (half grey, half white)
c) 6 grey mice, 6 white mice.

Q2 Sally can cross the plants. If the parent plant with red flowers is thoroughbred (RR) then all their offspring will be red. If the parent plant with red flowers is hybrid (Rr) then there will be an approximate 1 : 1 ratio of red to white offspring.

Q3 a)

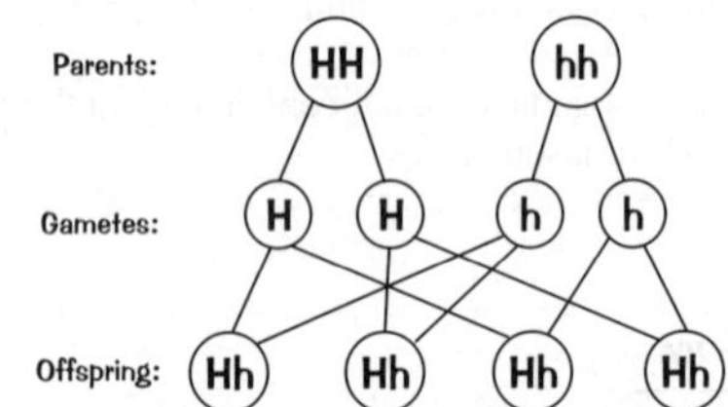

b) i) 1 / 100%
ii) 0

Q4 a) Because plenty of the family carry the allele but aren't sufferers.
b)

	Carrier	Sufferer
Libby	50%	25%
Anne	50%	0%

Q5 a) Dd. Polydactyly is a dominant disorder, so if Amy was DD she would have passed it on to all her children but Brook and Beth are unaffected.

Biology 2b — Enzymes and Genetics

b) i) Dd (Because Alan must be dd because he is not a sufferer. So to be polydactyl, Brian must have inherited Amy's D allele.)

ii)

		Carol	
		D	d
Brian	D	D D	D d
	d	D d	d d

iii) 25% (or 0.25 or ¼)

Pages 93-94 — Fossils

Q1 a) A fossil is the remains of an organism from many years ago.
b) Fossils are usually found in rocks.
Q2 bones, slowly, rock, shaped, clay, hardens, cast
Q3 a) i) A clear yellow 'stone' made from fossilised resin.
ii) There's no oxygen or moisture in amber, so decay microbes can't survive to decay dead organisms.
Thus, dead organisms are preserved.
b) No oxygen or moisture — Tar pits
Too acidic — Peat bogs
Too cold — Glaciers
Q4 E.g. many early life forms were soft bodied, so they decayed away completely without leaving fossils. Fossils that formed a very long time ago may have been destroyed by geological activity (like movement of tectonic plates).
Q5 a) The shell will eventually be replaced with minerals as the sediments around it turn to rock.
b) Fossil B is in a lower layer of rock. It's likely this layer formed first. Subsequent layers built up on top.
Q6 a) A hypothesis.
b) It was so long ago that it's now very difficult to find any conclusive evidence for the hypothesis or against it.
c) E.g. another theory suggests that life began in a primordial swamp. Simple organic molecules joined to make more complex ones which eventually joined to give life forms.

Pages 95-96 — Extinction and Speciation

Q1 a) Extinct species are those that once lived but that don't exist any more.
b) We mainly know about extinct animals because we have found fossils of them. Also accept: We know more about some animals like mammoths because early people drew pictures of them, or about dodos because people wrote descriptions of them.
Q2 A catastrophic event kills every member of the species — A rare plant that lives on the side of a volcano is wiped out when the volcano erupts.
The environment changes too quickly — An island's rainforest is completely chopped down, destroying the habitat of the striped monkey.
A new disease kills every member of the species — Every member of a species of toad is killed when a new fungal pathogen is accidentally introduced to their habitat.
Q3 a) The development of a new species.
b) Because populations of the same species have become so different that they can't interbreed to give fertile offspring.
c) true
Q4 1 — There are two populations of the same species.
2 — Physical barriers separate the populations.
3 — The populations adapt to their new environments.
4 — A new species develops.
Q5 a) The spiders may have out-competed the squirrels for food (bananas).
b) The gibbons may have been a new predator and hunted the squirrels.
Q6 a) Isolation is where populations of a species are separated.
b) 1. A physical barrier geographically isolates some individuals from the main population.
2. Conditions on either side of a physical barrier are slightly different.
3. Each population shows variation because they have a wide range of alleles.
4. In each population, individuals with characteristics that make them better adapted to their environment have a better chance of survival and so are more likely to breed successfully.
5. The alleles that control the beneficial characteristics are more likely to be passed on to the next generation.
6. Eventually, individuals from the different populations have changed so much that they become separate species.

Pages 97-100 — Mixed Questions — Biology 2b

Q1 a) Stem cells have the ability to differentiate into different types of cell.
b) i) mitosis
ii) Stem cells from embryos can differentiate into all the different types of cells in the human body.
c) Possible answer: Some people feel that using embryos for stem cell research is unethical; they feel that every embryo has a right to life.
Q2 a) White flowers
b) i) FF
ii) ff
iii) Ff
c) 3 purple:1 white, because he is crossing two purple flowers which both have the alleles Ff.
Q3 Recessive, because the parents carry the allele but do not show the characteristics of albinism themselves.
Q4 a)

Gg Gg
G g G g
GG Gg Gg gg

b) i) 3:1
ii) Because fertilisation is random, there is a 1 in 4 chance of each rabbit being white, but this is just a probability and the reality may be different.
c) All of their offspring will be white, because white rabbits are homozygous for the recessive allele (gg) and so cannot be carrying the allele for grey fur.
Q5 a) Fossil X
b) Most animals have hard parts in their bodies e.g. bones or shells. These parts are fossilised more easily.
c) If two organisms can reproduce and produce fertile offspring then they are of the same species. It is not possible to tell if two fossilised animals would have been able to do this.
Q6 a) E.g. her heart rate increased.
b) i) anaerobic respiration
ii) glucose → lactic acid (+ energy)
iii) She had an oxygen debt. She needed to breathe hard to get enough oxygen to oxidise the lactic acid.
c) i) amylase
ii) The salivary glands, the pancreas and the small intestine.
Q7 a) Really long molecules of DNA.
b) In humans, the males are XY and the females are XX.
Q8 a) The amount of DNA is doubling because the DNA is replicating itself.
b) The two daughter cells separate.
c) i) body cells
ii) asexual reproduction
d) E.g. mitosis involves one division whereas meiosis involves two divisions. / Mitosis produces two new cells whereas meiosis produces four new cells. / Mitosis produces identical cells whereas meiosis produces genetically different cells.

Biology 3a — Life Processes

Biology 3a — Life Processes

Pages 101-102 — Osmosis

Q1 a) side B

b) from B to A

c) The liquid level on side B will **fall**, because **water will flow from side B to side A by osmosis**.

Q2 a)

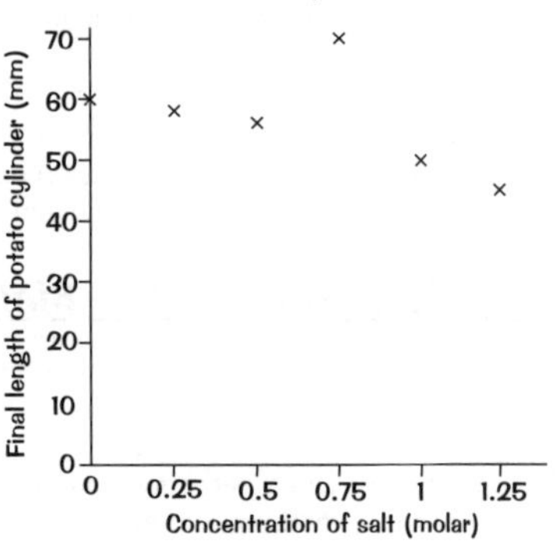

b)

Concentration of salt (molar)	Final length of potato cylinder (mm)	Change in length of potato cylinder (mm)
0	60	+10
0.25	58	+8
0.5	56	+6
0.75	70	+20
1	50	0
1.25	45	-5

c) i) 0.75 molar (it doesn't follow the pattern)

ii) Repeat the experiment at least twice more to find the most likely values.

d) Any three from, e.g: the volume of solution / the length of time the cylinders are left for / the surface area of the cylinders / the temperature.

Q3 a) tissue fluid

b) Water will move by osmosis from the tissue fluid into the body cells as the tissue fluid has a higher water concentration and the body cells have a lower water concentration.

c) The net movement of water molecules stops when there is an equal concentration of water molecules on either side of the membrane — when they have reached equilibrium.

Q4 a) Water molecules moved by osmosis from the pot (where they were in a higher concentration) to the meat (where they were in a lower concentration), thus adding size to the meat.

b) i) water / sugar solution

ii) It has come from inside the fruit by osmosis (to an area of lower water concentration where the sugar surrounds the fruit).

iii) The higher water concentration surrounding the fruit causes the movement of water from around the fruit to inside the fruit. This increases mass and makes the raisins and sultanas bigger.

Pages 103-104 — Gas and Solute Exchange

Q1 a)

Feature	Diffusion	Osmosis	Active transport
Substances move from areas of higher concentration to areas of lower concentration	✓	✓	
Requires energy			✓

b) Osmosis involves the movement of **water**.

Q2 a) True

b) True

c) False

d) False

e) True

f) False

Q3 a) A water vapour / oxygen
B water vapour / oxygen
C carbon dioxide

b) diffusion

c) It's controlled by guard cells, which open and close the stomata to allow or prevent the gases diffusing in and out.

d) 1. The underside of the leaf.
2. The walls of the cells within the leaf.

e) It increases the surface area of the leaf, which increases its effectiveness at gas exchange / means it can collect more light for a given volume.

Q4 gases, dissolved, maximise, thin, short, large, blood, ventilated, bigger, complex, long

Q5 a)

Plant	In a room (% change in mass)	Next to a fan (% change in mass)	By a lamp (% change in mass)	Next to a fan and by a lamp (% change in mass)
1	5	8	10	13
2	5	9	11	15
3	4	11	9	13
Average	**4.7**	**9.3**	**10**	**13.7**

b) next to a fan and by a lamp

c) To improve the accuracy of her results / make them more reliable.

d) Less water would have been lost since most water loss occurs through stomata that are located mainly on the undersides of leaves.

e)

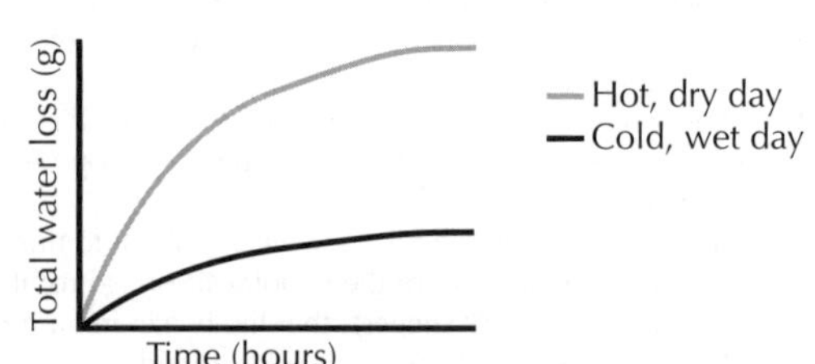

Page 105 — The Breathing System

Q1 a) The movement of air into and out of the lungs.

b) It's needed so that oxygen from the air can diffuse into the bloodstream (and to the cells for respiration) and so that carbon dioxide can diffuse out of the blood.

Q2 a)

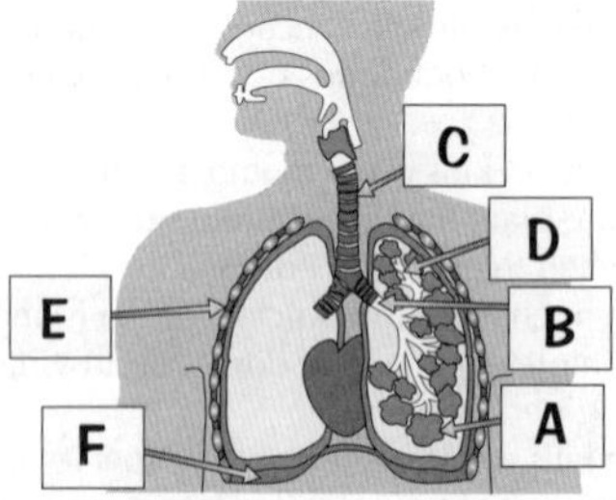

b) i) in, intercostal, diaphragm, flattens, up, out, increase, fall, drawn into

ii) relax, ribcage, down, in, volume, decreases, rises, forced out of

Q3 a) A machine that moves air into or out of the lungs.

b) Air is pumped into the lungs, which expands the ribcage. When it stops pumping, the ribcage relaxes and pushes air back out of the lungs.

Page 106 — Diffusion Through Cell Membranes

Q1a) E.g. the alveoli of the lungs, the villi of the small intestine / ileum

b) E.g. oxygen and digested food (glucose)

Biology 3a — Life Processes

Q2 a)

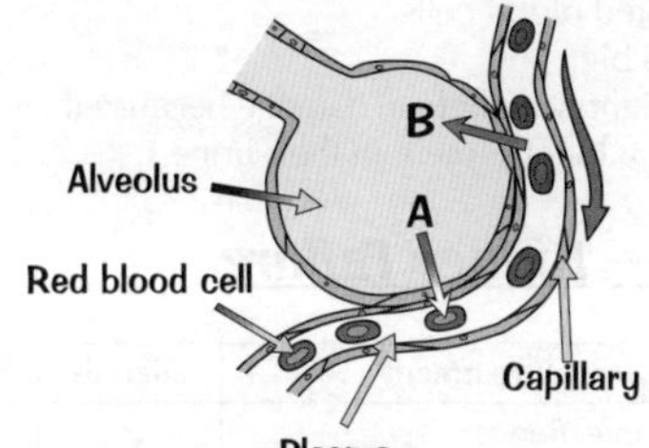

b) A: oxygen
B: carbon dioxide

c) diffusion

Q3 a)

Size (cm)	Surface area (cm^2)	Time taken for dye uptake (s)
1 x 1 x 1	**6**	41.6
2 x 2 x 2	**24**	9.3
5 x 5 x 5	**150**	1.7
10 x 10 x 10	**600**	0.4

b) i) bigger
ii) increases

c) Villi provide a greater surface area in the gut. As this increases the rate of uptake increases, so nutrients are absorbed more quickly.

d) E.g. a good blood supply

Page 107 — Active Transport

Q1 a) False
b) True
c) True

Q2 a) root hair cell
b) Absorbing water and mineral ions from the soil.
c) The soil generally has a lower concentration of minerals than the root hair cells. Diffusion only takes place from areas of higher concentration to areas of lower concentration.
d) The concentration of minerals in the soil is lower than in root hair cells. The cells use active transport to absorb the minerals. This requires energy, which is released by respiration.

Q3 a) Any two from, e.g: add the same concentration of potassium ions to the solutions initially / use the same amount of solution / use the same size/mass of barley seedling / examine the seedlings for the same amount of time.
b) X. The seedling that has taken up the more potassium ions grows better.
c) 7.5 units

Page 108 — Water Flow Through Plants

Q1 a) b) c) E.g.

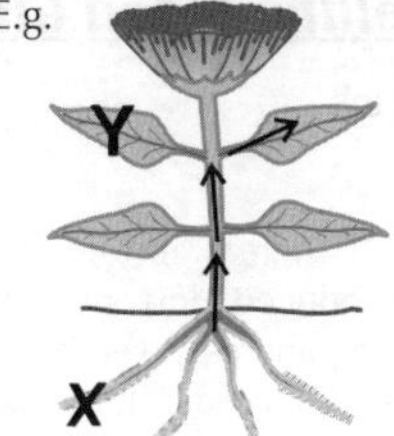

Q2 leaves, evaporation/diffusion, diffusion/evaporation, leaf, xylem, roots, transpiration stream

Q3 a) xylem, phloem
b) i) xylem
ii) roots, stem/leaves, leaves/stem
c) i) phloem
ii) leaves, growing, storage

Pages 109-110 — Circulatory System — The Heart

Q1 a) False
b) True
c) True
d) False

Q2 a) pulmonary artery
b) vena cava
c) right atrium
d) right ventricle
e) aorta
f) pulmonary vein
g) valves
h) left ventricle
i) To prevent the backflow of blood.
j) double, heart, lungs, oxygenated, deoxygenated

Q3 E.g. function 1: Delivering substances to cells.
Substances transported: glucose and oxygen.
E.g. function 2: Removing waste products.
Substances transported: carbon dioxide and urea.

Q4 atria, ventricles, ventricles, out, organs, arteries, veins

Q5 A: Pulmonary artery
B: Aorta
C: Vena cava
D: Pulmonary vein

Page 111 — Circulatory System — Blood Vessels

Q1 a) The walls are only one cell thick to allow substances to pass through more easily / there is a shorter distance for diffusion.
b) oxygen, carbon dioxide
c) E.g. glucose/food

Q2 a) Artery – A , Vein — B
b) i) Arteries carry blood away from the heart at high pressure so they need to be strong and able to stretch and spring back.
ii) Veins carry blood back to the heart at low pressure. Valves prevent the blood flowing back in the wrong direction.

Q3 a) E.g. the vein has a wider lumen / thinner wall / valves.
b) The length of the blood vessel, because this is the dependent variable.
c) The vein, because it has a thinner wall.
d) To make his experiment a fair test (the vessels are the same age, etc.)

Page 112 — Circulatory System — The Blood

Q1 a) False
b) False
c) False
d) True
e) True
f) False
g) True

Q2 a) i) haemoglobin
ii) oxyhaemoglobin
b) $365 / 120 \approx 3$

Q3 They engulf microorganisms and break them down.
They produce antibodies that attack microorganisms.
They produce antitoxins to neutralise the toxins produced by microorganisms.

Q4 a) E.g. red blood cells, white blood cells, platelets, glucose, amino acids, carbon dioxide, urea, hormones, antibodies, antitoxins.

b)

Substance	Travelling from	Travelling to
Urea	Liver	Kidneys
Carbon dioxide	Organs / cells	Lungs
Glucose	Gut / small intestine	Organs / cells

Biology 3a — Life Processes

Page 113 — Circulation Aids

Q1 tubes, arteries, narrow, open, muscles, beating, heart attack, coronary, irritate, scar tissue, clotting

Q2 a) C
b) D
c) B
d) A

Q3 a) E.g. it won't be rejected by the body's immune system.
b) Any two from, e.g: surgery to fit an artificial heart can lead to bleeding and infection. / Artificial hearts don't work as well as healthy natural ones — parts of the heart could wear out or the electrical motor could fail. / Blood doesn't flow through artificial hearts as smoothly, which can cause blood clots and lead to strokes. / The patient may have to take drugs to thin their blood, which can cause problems with bleeding if they're hurt in an accident.

Page 114 — Homeostasis

Q1 Homeostasis is the maintenance of a constant internal environment.

Q2 a) via the lungs when you breathe out
b) E.g. urea

Q3 a) The thermoregulatory centre in the brain detects the temperature of the blood.
b) from temperature receptors in the skin

Q4 a)

	Too hot	Too cold
hair	hairs lie down flat	hairs stand up
sweat glands	more sweat produced	less sweat produced
blood vessels	dilate near skin	constrict near skin

b) When you shiver, muscles contract automatically. This needs respiration, which releases some energy to warm the body.

Page 115 — The Kidneys and Homeostasis

Q1 a) False
b) True
c) True
d) False
e) True

Q2 a) They're taken into the body in food and drink, and then absorbed into the blood.
b) E.g. too much or too little water would be drawn into the cells, which would damage the cells / so the cells wouldn't work properly.

Q3

	Do you sweat **a lot** or **a little**?	Is the amount of urine you produce **high** or **low**?	Is the urine you produce **more** or **less** concentrated?
Hot Day	A lot	low	more
Cold Day	A little	high	less

Q4 a) i) ions, sugar
ii) Ions — to replace those lost in sweat.
Sugar — to replace the sugar that's used up by muscles during exercise.
b) E.g. whether a scientific study has been carried out that's published in a reputable journal.

Page 116 — Kidney Function

Q1 E, B, D, C, A

Q2 a) i) ions, water, sugar, urea
ii) ions, water, sugar
iii) ions (excess), water (excess), urea
b) Active transport is used to absorb ions and sugar.
Water moves by osmosis (a special type of diffusion).

c) i) protein and red blood cells
ii) They are too big.

Q3 Subject 2 might have kidney damage because they have glucose and a lot of protein in their urine.

Pages 117-118 — Kidney Failure

Q1

Feature of treatment	Dialysis	Transplant
High risk of infection	✓	✓
Long-term, one-off treatment		✓
Patient can lead a relatively normal life		✓
Patient must take drugs		✓
Patient usually needs to live near a hospital	✓	

Q2 a) i) proteins and red blood cells
ii) They are too big to fit through the membrane, so they will remain in the blood.
b) urea
c) It is equal to prevent the diffusion of glucose out of the bloodstream and into the fluid, as it would then be lost from the patient's body.

Q3 a) Because the antigens are foreign / not recognised by the patient's body.
b) E.g. a donor with a tissue type that closely matches the patient is chosen. The patient takes drugs to suppress their immune system.

Q4 a) 1. A needle is inserted into a blood vessel in the patient's arm to remove blood.
2. The patient's blood flows into the dialysis machine and between partially permeable membranes that are surrounded by dialysis fluid.
3. Excess water, ions and wastes are filtered out of the blood and pass into the dialysis fluid.
4. Dialysis continues until nearly all the waste and excess substances are removed.
5. Blood is returned to the patient's body using a vein in their arm.
b) So that useful dissolved ions won't be lost from the blood during dialysis (by diffusion).
c) To keep the concentrations of dissolved substances in the blood at normal levels.

Q5 a) and **b)**

	Year	
	2004	**2013**
Total number of patients with kidney failure	37 000	68 000
Number receiving dialysis	20 500	**38 000**
Number that have received a transplant	**16 500**	30 000

c) i) 30 000 – (20 000 + 6500) = £3500
ii) (30 000 × 3) – (20 000 + (6500 × 3)) = £50 500

Pages 119-120 — Controlling Blood Glucose

Q1 a) from digested food and drink
b) E.g. pancreas
c) insulin and glucagon

Q2 Missing words are: insulin, pancreas, insulin, liver, glycogen, glucose, blood, reduced / lower.

Q3 Glucagon is secreted by the pancreas. This makes the liver turn glycogen into glucose. Glucose is added by the liver into the blood. So the blood glucose level increases.

Q4 a) A condition where the pancreas produces little or no insulin so a person's blood sugar level can get too high.
b) By injecting insulin at meal times, by avoiding foods that are rich in carbohydrate, by exercising after eating meals.

Q5 a) i) Diabetics used to use insulin from animals such as pigs. Now they can use human insulin produced by genetically modified bacteria.
ii) It doesn't cause adverse reactions in patients, like animal insulin did.

Biology 3b — Humans and Their Environment

b) i) A pancreas transplant.
ii) E.g. risk of rejecting the organ, having to take immunosuppressive drugs.
c) E.g. artificial pancreases, using stem cells

Page 121 — Mixed Questions — Biology 3a

Q1 a) E.g. a large surface area for diffusion to occur. A moist lining for dissolving gases. Very thin walls so there's a short distance for substance to diffuse across. A good blood supply to get stuff into and out of the blood quickly.
b) i) red blood cells
ii) haemoglobin
iii) They have a large surface area for absorbing oxygen. They have no nucleus to make more room for haemoglobin (which carries oxygen).
Q2 a) root hair cell
b) It gives the cell a large surface area.
c) Minerals are absorbed by active transport, whereas water is not. If respiration stops there will be no energy to power active transport, so no minerals will be absorbed.
d) i) It escapes by diffusion.
ii) hot, dry and windy conditions
iii) oxygen, (allow CO_2 at night)

Biology 3b — Humans and Their Environment

Pages 122-123 — Human Impact on the Environment

Q1 a) bigger
b) faster
c) greater
Q2 a) i) John is more likely to live in the UK and Derek in Kenya.
ii) The following should be ticked:
John buys more belongings, which use more raw materials to manufacture.
John has central heating in his home but Derek has a wood fire.
John drives a car and Derek rides a bicycle.
b) Any sensible suggestion, such as: John could use his car less, use his central heating less, recycle more waste, buy fewer new things, etc.
Q3 a) i) Decrease
ii) E.g. there will be less land for the voles to build their nests on. / The voles will have less of the resources they need, like food and water.
b) Any two from: e.g. building / dumping waste / quarrying
Q4 a)

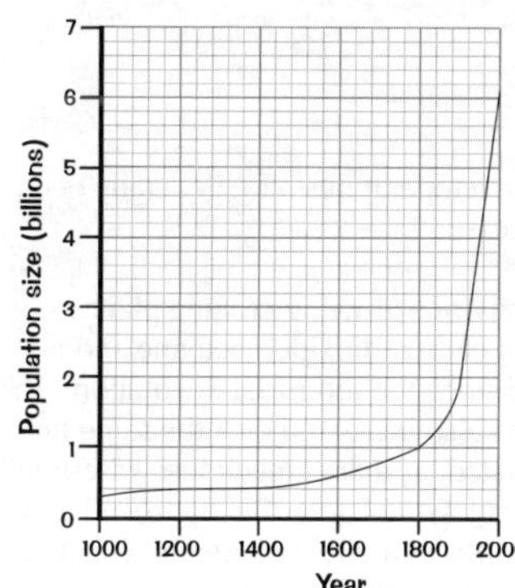

b) Any 2 from: Improvements in medicine meant that fewer people died of diseases. More efficient farming methods produced more food so fewer people died of hunger. Living standards improved over much of the world. Hygiene and sanitation improved over much of the world, etc.
c) It means we are producing more waste.

Q5 a) E.g. pesticides/insecticides, herbicides/weedkillers, fertilisers.
b) E.g. these chemicals can build up on land and might not be easily broken down. The excess may wash into rivers and lakes and pollute the water. These chemicals can harm living things.

Page 124 — Carbon Dioxide and the Greenhouse Effect

Q1 carbon dioxide, burning, global warming, sequestered, oceans, less
Q2 The greenhouse effect is needed for life on Earth as we know it.
Increasing amounts of greenhouse gases cause global warming.
Q3 a) The greenhouses gases absorb much of the heat that is radiated away from Earth and re-radiate it in all directions. This keeps the atmosphere relatively warm.
b) All the energy radiated out by the Earth would be lost. This means that the Earth would be much colder.
c) More greenhouse gas in the atmosphere means that more of the Sun's heat is trapped rather than radiated back out into space. This means the Earth gets warmer.

Page 125 — Deforestation and the Destruction of Peat Bogs

Q1 a) During deforestation, trees are burnt to clear the land, releasing carbon dioxide into the air. Microorganisms feed on bits of dead wood that remain and release carbon dioxide as they respire. Trees take in carbon dioxide for use in photosynthesis, so if there are fewer trees less carbon dioxide is absorbed from the atmosphere.
b) i) false
ii) true
c) E.g. to provide timber for building, to produce paper from wood.
Q2 a) The variety of different species in a habitat.
b) We could miss out on things like new medicines, foods or fibres.
Q3 a) Plants that live in bogs don't fully decay when they die, because there's not enough oxygen. The partly-rotted plants build up to form peat.
b) Carbon is stored in the dead plants that make up the peat. As a bog is drained, the peat starts to decompose and carbon dioxide is released.
c) Use peat-free compost to reduce the demand for peat.

Page 126 — Climate Change

Q1 1. Higher temperatures make ice melt.
2. Sea levels start to rise.
3. Low-lying areas are at risk of flooding.
Q2 a) reduce
b) north
c) cooler, less
d) extreme
Q3 They might be right, but we can't know for sure from such small amounts of evidence. Both students would need to carry out long-term studies using a lot more data.
Q4 a) evidence: data that either supports or contradicts a particular hypothesis.
hypothesis: a possible explanation for a set of observations.
b) E.g. snow and ice cover, the temperature of the sea surface, the speed and the direction of ocean currents, atmospheric temperatures.

Biology 3b — Humans and Their Environment

Page 127 — Biofuels

Q1 a) respiration
b) anaerobic
c) ethanol
d) Ethanol
Q2 a) E.g. glucose
b) E.g. sugar cane / maize
Q3 generator, batch, waste, carbohydrates, fermented, heating, turbine
Q4 a) methane and carbon dioxide
b) E.g. any two from: human sewage, animal dung, kitchen waste (e.g. vegetable peelings), agricultural / plant waste (e.g. fallen leaves), sludge waste from factories (e.g. sugar factories)

Pages 128-129 — Using Biogas Generators

Q1 a) Waste material is being fermented / broken down by the anaerobic respiration of microorganisms.
b) The balloon will inflate.
c) The microorganisms will grow faster (and produce more biogas) at a warmer temperature.
Q2 a) About 45 °C.
b) E.g. because heat will be produced during the process.
c) E.g. any two from: amount of waste, amount of bacteria, surface area / size of waste particles, pH, presence of toxins
d) The toxins would poison the microorganisms and inhibit the breakdown of the material.
Q3 a) batch
b) continuous
c) all the time
d) continuous
Q4 a) i) So that the houses are not near the smell.
ii) It will be easier to transport animal dung to the generator.
iii) To keep it warm so the microorganisms can work effectively.
b) E.g. any two from: lower cost fuel, it disposes of their waste, improves the properties of the dung as a fertiliser, less disease and pollution from waste, no need to spend hours collecting wood for fuel.
Q5 a) Energy from the Sun was incorporated into plants by photosynthesis. Some of this energy is then passed to animals when they eat the plants.
b) i) Although it produces carbon dioxide, it is derived from recent photosynthesis, which used up the same amount of carbon dioxide. So, there's no net production of carbon dioxide.
ii) E.g. doesn't produce significant amounts of sulfur dioxide or nitrous oxides which cause acid rain. / Burning methane means it's not released into the atmosphere to contribute to global warming. / Waste is removed which would otherwise cause pollution and disease.

Page 130 — Managing Food Production

Q1 a) Wheat → Human
b) There are fewer steps in this food chain so less energy is lost.
Q2 a) *Fusarium*
b) fermenters, glucose syrup, oxygen, purified
Q3 a) The animals are kept close together, indoors and in small pens, so they're warm and can't move about.
b) The pigs don't waste energy on movement or give out much energy as heat. So the transfer of energy from the feed to the pigs is more efficient — they grow faster on less food.
c) E.g. the pork is cheaper.

Page 131 — Problems With Food Production and Distribution

Q1 a)

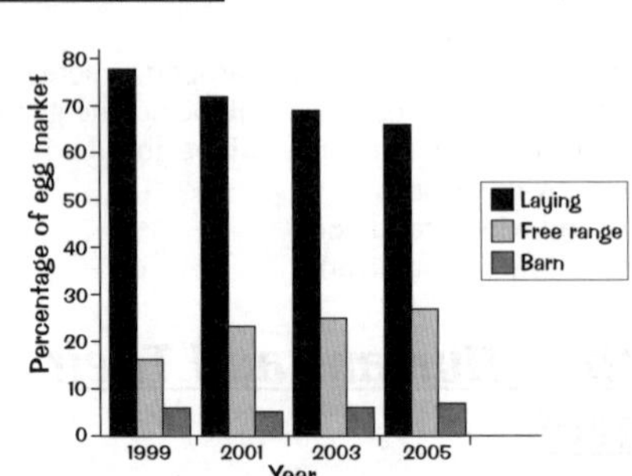

b) Laying −12%
Barn 1%
Free range 11%
c) E.g. more people are choosing not to buy eggs that have been produced by hens kept in distressing conditions / more people choose to buy eggs produced by hens kept in healthy conditions because they're concerned for the hens' wellbeing / more people believe that eggs produced by healthy, free range chickens will taste better
Q2 Products with lots of food miles are transported a long way from where they're produced to where they're sold. This means burning fossil fuels, which releases carbon dioxide into the atmosphere, contributing to global warming.
Q3 a) Fishing quotas put limits on the number and size of fish that can be caught in certain areas. This prevents certain species from being overfished.
b) Having enough food without using resources faster than they renew.

Page 132 — Mixed Questions — Biology 3b

Q1 a) i) crowded, easy
ii) antibiotics
iii) increases
b) biogas
Q2 a) Average surface temperatures have generally been increasing since 1859.
b) i) Methane.
ii) E.g. cow rearing / rice growing / rotting plants.
c) The amounts of carbon dioxide, methane and nitrous oxide have increased since the Industrial Revolution. The global temperature has also increased over the same time. The two may be related, as extra greenhouse gases will absorb more heat, warming the Earth. But there's no definite proof in these two graphs of a direct cause and effect relationship between the two variables.